Praise for *A Ready Hope*

"When the biggest high school massacre in U.S. history happened at Columbine High School on April 20, 1999, we who were caught up in being ground zero caregivers had no manual on our shelves. Today that would be different. Haueisen and Flores have written a well informed and passionately faithful resource that should be on every pastor's book shelf, as well as those congregational leaders responsible for community outreach. Haueisen and Flores not only "get it" when speaking about the myriad of emotional and spiritual storms that engulf all people in the aftermath of such a tragedy, they provide compelling hope and practical steps for those who must care."

Rick Barger, Pastor, Epiphany Lutheran Church, Suwanee, Georgia, and former Lead Pastor, Abiding Hope Lutheran Church, Littleton, Colorado

"While preparing for a disaster is logical and critical to a quick and effective response, sometimes the best thing one can do is pull up a chair and listen to the disaster narrative that so desperately needs to be heard. Haueisen and Flores provide the reader, however, with a practical approach to disaster response that leaves one both prepared and equipped to respond. Whether read by a group or individuals who want to be part of the solution, Haueisen and Flores provide suggestions and guidelines which, when implemented, will make a difference in the lives of individuals affected by disaster."

Rev. Lynn Hyder, M.Div., BCC, Staff Chaplain, The McFarland Institute, New Orleans, Louisiana

"In the post-9/11, post-Katrina world, communities are more aware than ever that none are immune to the impact of domestic disaster. "Tried by fire" through a succession of hurricanes, Haueisen and Flores have written a practical guide to disaster response and recovery ministry. Study it now—then make it part of your community's disaster response kit."

Richard Bruesehoff, Director for Lifelong Learning, Evangelical Lutheran Church in America, and author of Clergy Renewal: The Alban Guide to Sabbatical Planning

"Haueisen and Flores listen in and through disasters. They help us see the 'invisible work' of faith communities that respond to domestic disaster. Parishes that decide that recovery work is not their calling will also find this book a valuable resource to discern what their community role should be."

The Very Reverend Dr. James A. Kowalski, Dean, The Cathedral Church of Saint John the Divine

A Ready Hope

A Ready Hope

EFFECTIVE DISASTER MINISTRY FOR CONGREGATIONS

Kathryn M. Haueisen
and
Carol H. Flores

Herndon, Virginia
www.alban.org

The Alban Institute
2121 Cooperative Way, Suite 100
Herndon, VA 20171

Cover design by Tobias Becker, Bird Box Design.

Library of Congress Cataloging-in-Publication Data

Haueisen, Kathryn M.
A ready hope: effective disaster ministry for congregations / Kathryn M. Haueisen and Carol Flores.
p. cm.
Includes bibliographical references.
ISBN 978-1-56699-386-9
1. Church work with disaster victims. 2. Disaster relief. 3. Social service--Religious aspects--Christianity. I. Flores, Carol. II. Title.
HV554.4.H38 2009
363.34'575--dc22

2009004441

13 12 11 10 09 VP 1 2 3 4 5

Dedicated to
the many faithful men, women, and youth
who reveal the love of God
by their service in times of disaster

Contents

Foreword

What do you do when disaster strikes? Some of us have a plan for escaping our homes in a fire, though too many of us do not. Very few of us have a plan for action if a major disaster—a flood or hurricane-force storm—were to hit our homes. Even those who live in frequently storm-struck areas do not always plan ahead.

Congregations often fail to plan ahead as well. While many have a fire drill plan to evacuate the building, few are prepared to handle major disasters—either to their own church building, their church members' homes and businesses, or to their community as a whole. This book will help to remedy that situation.

Many churches serve their communities with various programs, such as day care centers and food pantries, and perhaps occasionally offer overnight facilities to the homeless, but most are not ready for serious calamities. How many congregations are prepared to serve as Red Cross shelters in disaster areas? How many would know how to function as a Point of Distribution (POD) for the Federal Emergency Management Agency (FEMA)? How many even have a plan to communicate with each other and care for their most vulnerable members when electricity, land lines, and cell phone systems all fail?

The truth is that many more congregations *should* be prepared to do these things, since disasters happen all the time, and the Red Cross and other organizations depend on people, resources, and facilities for disaster relief. Who better to provide relief than those who know how important it is to find a "shelter in the time of storm," to quote an old hymn. Those who trust in God as their "refuge and strength, an ever-present help in trouble" (Psalm 46:1) are the ones who ought to extend that help to their neighbors, especially in times of disaster and difficulty.

In this volume Kathy Haueisen and Carol Flores provide guidance for churches in providing disaster ministry—help for knowing what to do, how to help, and how to make decisions in the midst of a disaster. They give sound advice all the way from practical details—like keeping an old phone on hand to plug in when the power goes out and cordless phones don't work—to wisdom for leaders regarding how to stay calm in the face of the storms—both natural and psychological—that they, their church and their community may face.

All this good advice, accompanied by sidebars and appendices of important information, comes through an engaging story of one congregation's experience of a natural disaster and its aftermath. The authors tell about the difficulties and decisions this church faces each step of the way. The dire effects of disaster on a community over weeks and months are detailed, as well as the church's response at various stages—all the way to considering an ongoing ministry for disaster relief from their congregation to other regions. Readers will soon come to care deeply about the characters in this story and be caught up in the perplexing problems and decisions they face. This excellent resource book is also a page-turning story.

Congregations will find this book to be a rich resource for disaster relief ministry in their own communities and beyond. Though no church wishes for a disaster to strike, all should be prepared for one. Churches not only are places that people naturally turn to for help in times of crisis; they also are called to provide the help they can as servants for good in the world.

In addition to specific advice for hosting a Red Cross shelter or a FEMA Point of Distribution, the authors also provide wisdom for dealing with people and organizations in all stages of a disaster—

before, during, and long afterward as the cleanup and rebuilding continues. They reveal the decision-making processes required for many issues, from personal to congregational to denominational choices in the wake of a disaster. And they give advice for spiritual care and counsel through the worship and the volunteers of the congregation, knowing that in crisis people need to gather together and need the ritual of worship to calm their hearts and lift their spirits.

Some of the wonderful examples of service in this book can be adopted by churches who are not in the midst of a crisis but could help those who are, such as the "how I can help" offering, in which church members put slips of paper with their contributions of skill into the offering plate.

Also included are helpful plans for dealing with interchurch relationships and combined community services, as well as wise words for leaders to take care of themselves and their families in the midst of disaster follow-up. Moreover, churches who send volunteers and groups on servant trips can learn much from this book about how to be good volunteers who actually do contribute selflessly to those in need.

Church members and church leaders who read this book will want to adopt one of the basic principles of this book, and of disaster response teams: "Start where you are. Use what resources you have. Just do what you can." And as they do so, they will be fulfilling the call of the prophet Micah to "do justice, love kindness, and walk humbly with your God." This book will teach humble leaders how to serve God in mighty ways.

Rev. Kathleen Smith
Author, *Stilling the Storm: Worship and Congregational Leadership in Difficult Times*

Preface

For I was hungry and you gave me something to eat,
I was thirsty and you gave me something to drink,
I was a stranger and you invited me in.
—Matthew 25:35

A variety of storms blew through our family beginning at the dawn of the twenty-first century. Some of these were of the "act of God" variety—the tropical storms and hurricanes that have recently battered the Gulf Coast on a regular basis. We both live in Houston. New Orleans is part of our denomination's regional judicatory. Most recently, Hurricane Ike has played havoc in our community. Our backgrounds in volunteer and paid ministries within the Lutheran and ecumenical communities have drawn us both into disaster-response work. We have different experiences and different motivations for engaging in this ministry, but we share these things:

- A sharp learning curve about the mostly invisible world of domestic disaster-recovery work within the faith communities.
- A deep appreciation for the selfless men and women who enter the chaos of disaster sites to do what they can to restore safety, sanity, hope, and dignity amid pain and suffering.
- A passion to support the efforts of disaster-recovery personnel and to find the resources they need to do their jobs.
- A determination to educate others, so that they will be prepared when disaster comes their way and better able to support the work of disaster responders.

Disaster response and recovery ministry is an amazing story of God's people carrying out God's mission. In Micah 6:8b we hear God's agenda for people of faith: "And what does the LORD require of you? To act justly and to love mercy and to walk humbly with your God." Humility is a great resource in a disaster area. The most effective disaster-response volunteers are those who come willing to learn.

Mark 12:30 records Jesus's answer when he was asked what was the greatest commandment: "The most important one, Love the LORD your God with all your heart and with all your soul and with all your mind and with all your strength. The second is this: 'Love your neighbor as yourself.' There is no commandment greater than these." Disaster-response ministry is God's love made visible through hundreds of small deeds—from handing someone a drink of water or a clean face mask to hauling out one trash bag of debris after another.

Matthew 25:35 addresses the most basic human needs: "For I was hungry and you gave me food, I was thirsty and you gave me something to drink, I was a stranger and you welcomed me, I was naked and you gave me clothing, . . . I was in prison and you visited to me" (NRSV). Survivors of disasters need food, water, clothing, and a sense of hope amid nightmarish frustration, red tape, and shortages of everything.

Here's how each of us came to be involved.

Kathy's Story

When Katrina devastated New Orleans, I was serving as pastor of a congregation in central Houston. From the third floor of our office area, I could see the Reliant Center, where the buses brought the terrified and desperate survivors of flooded New Orleans. At the time, I was in recovery mode myself from some personal losses. I was ready and determined to do something for someone else in need. Katrina, in August 2005, and a few weeks later Rita, in September, offered that opportunity.

Getting involved in the recovery efforts following these hurricanes has shown me how much I needed to know about disaster response and recovery ministry. Before the 2005 hurricanes I generally felt great empathy for those who experienced disasters. Like thousands of others, I wrote checks to disaster-response organizations, offered prayers, and discussed the causes and the causalities of disasters with my colleagues. I sent and took youth groups on mission trips to disaster areas to help with the tedious process of cleaning up.

Still, I had no idea how much I didn't know about the amazing—but virtually invisible—ecumenical faith-based network in place throughout the United States. Hundreds of men and women are ready, willing, and more than able to respond almost instantly to the worst disasters we hear about. Each of the organizations affiliated with this network has access to thousands of volunteers ready to travel hundreds of miles at great personal expense and inconvenience to help as needed. I had no idea.

For example, in the wake of Hurricane Ike, the city of Houston hosted more than eight thousand power-company employees from thirty-two states. True, these people were on a payroll, but many made enormous sacrifices and put their lives in danger to restore power to this Gulf Coast region. They worked from 5:00 A.M. to 9:00 P.M. every day to get the city fully powered again. Some left their own homes in need of repair to restore power in areas that came through the storm with little more than yard cleanup to worry about.

My conversations with clergy colleagues and lay members of faith communities indicate that many of us "have no idea." We who are members of faith-based organizations need to know. Both governmental and nongovernmental organizations turn to us to help them help others. We have a vital and unique part to play, but too many of us haven't learned our parts well enough. A variety of organizations bring help into a disaster area. Faith-based organizations also bring hope. We bring both help and hope directly to the survivors of the disaster and to the other rescue and relief workers who leave home to assist. To maximize our efforts, we need to know what to expect after a disaster.

My hope is that this book will help people of faith to prepare themselves, their loved ones, and their faith community members for a disaster—and, in doing so, to equip themselves to be part of God's heart and hands on the long road to recovery when a disaster occurs.

Early on in my introduction to disaster recovery work, I learned this motto: *Start where you are. Use what you have. Do what you can.* Good advice. Only a handful of us will be called into full-time action when a disaster happens. However, the supporting roles the rest of us play can make all the difference to those who are called to this mission field.

Carol's Story

When the Challenger shuttle exploded in 1986, I was a fifteen-year-old high-school student in Clear Lake, Texas, the home of NASA. The father of one of my friends was the pilot of that mission. I still remember how profoundly that event affected me. It was frustrating to watch people hurt and not to know how to be a part of the healing.

When Tropical Storm Allison flooded Houston in 2001, I was a young mother caught up in the day-to-day life of three young children. Thirty-five families in our congregation had water in their homes. As congregation members, we did the best we could to help them begin cleaning up, but I remember the frustration of not knowing how to be more helpful for the long term. Later on in the recovery, I had a chance to lead a one-week day camp to help children deal with the emotional trauma that comes with disaster. I enjoyed the experience, but when it was over I was quite content to get back to the business of being a mom.

When Hurricanes Katrina and Rita struck the Gulf Coast, I was minding my own business, a beginning graduate student at the University of Houston. I was very much aware of the events unfolding around me but also caught up in my new grad-school endeavor. Several months later, out of nowhere, came the offer to be involved in the recovery. I was asked to lead the same children's program I had led after Allison— except that this time there would be fifty programs in eight weeks across the Texas and Louisiana Gulf Coast. Saying yes to that offer changed the focus of my graduate school work and the direction of my career.

It seems that I have often been near disaster but rarely directly affected—good fortune for which I am thankful. Since my involvement with Katrina and Rita, however, I find myself drawn to the tireless work done by so many in the wake of disaster. The countless numbers of professionals and volunteers who give hours, weeks, and months of their time doing thankless tasks never ceases to amaze me. And as a person involved with a faith community, I am aware how little our congregations know about the systems in place to respond to disaster. I have seen faith communities step up time and again to help others. But I have also seen frustration, anger, and hurt when toes get stepped on, cries for help seem to be ignored, or offers to help go unanswered.

My hope is that this book will focus the passion that communities of faith have for people in need and endow individuals with the resources needed to be effective in disaster ministry.

Acknowledgments

While it's always a risk that people will be overlooked in preparing a list of acknowledgments, nonetheless we wish to thank the following people for their support and help in the preparation of this book:

The Rev. Dr. Walt Ehrhardt, pastoral counselor in New Orleans

Bishop Michael Rinehart, bishop of the Texas-Louisiana Gulf Coast Synod of the Evangelical Lutheran Church in America

The Rev. Kevin Massey, executive director of Lutheran Disaster Response

The many, many people of the Gulf Coast who have given so much of themselves, even when their own lives have been torn apart by disasters

Rabbi Stephen Roberts and the Rev. Willard W. C. Ashley, co-authors of Disaster Spiritual Care: Practical Clergy Responses to Community, Regional and National Tragedy (Woodstock, Vt.: Skylight Paths, 2008)

Mary Woodward, Lutheran Disaster Response Ohio disaster coordinator

The Rev. Beth Gaede, editor for the Alban Institute (and patient, charming, gracious, competent, and all-around decent human being)

Dr. Kurt Senske, CEO of Lutheran Social Services of the South

The staff of Lutheran Social Services Disaster Response

The Rev. Ron Warren, retired bishop of the Evangelical Lutheran Church in America–Southeastern Synod and currently liaison to Lutheran synods and districts on behalf of Lutheran Disaster Response

Jennifer Posten, coordinator for disaster preparedness and response for Interfaith Ministries of Greater Houston, and chair of the Texas Gulf Coast Regional VOAD

The Rev. Tom Minor, retired U.S. Air Force chaplain

The Rev. Charles Lane, director for the ELCA Stewardship Key Leader program and former synod staff member during the flooding of the Grand Forks, North Dakota, region in 1997

The many men and women who are partners through Voluntary Organizations Active in Disaster (VOAD) for their patience in answering the many questions related to disaster response

Our families, who endured long hours of neglect as we completed this project and indulged our compassion and compulsion to be part of the solution to the disasters in our region: Dr. John Cashen and Rudy, Chris, Sarah, and Laura Flores

Thank you, one and all!

Acronyms for Common Disaster Response Terms

These are common usages in disaster response work. Of course, some acronyms may have more than one meaning.

ARC	American Red Cross
DHAP	Disaster Housing Assistance Program
DRC	Disaster Recovery Center
EMT	emergency medical technician
FBO	faith-based organization
FEMA	Federal Emergency Management Agency
HUD	Department of Housing and Urban Development
LTR C/O	long-term recovery committee/organization
NGO	nongovernmental organization
NHC	National Hurricane Center
NVOAD	National Voluntary Organizations Active in Disaster
NWS	National Weather Service
OEM	Office of Emergency Management
OSHA	Occupational Safety and Health Administration

POD	point of distribution
SAR	search and rescue
SBA	Small Business Administration
TSA	The Salvation Army
USAR	urban search and rescue
VAL	voluntary ageny liaison
VOAD	Voluntary Organizations Active in Disaster

This is only a sampling of acronyms. Not included on this list are all of the national faith-based disaster response organizations. Like any other specialized endeavor, disaster response has its own language, which can be overwhelming as the acronyms fly around in meetings and conversations. Newcomers can play an important role by asking for clarification of terms and acronyms to remind those who have been around awhile to slow down and translate more often.

Who's Who in Caldwell

In the course of reading this book you will meet the people of Caldwell, a midsize community in the Midwest. Caldwell and all who dwell there are fictional, created for the purpose of telling a story about how a disaster could affect a community and and its citizens. The details of this fictional account are based on actual people and situations the authors have encountered while doing disaster response ministry. The Emanuel Disaster Prepare and Respond team (DPR) is also fictitious, although it is based on a congregational team formed by a real congregation. Emanuel belongs to a fictional national church organization, which has a fictitious national Disaster Response Organization as well, abbreviated as DRO.

THE ALBRIGHT FAMILY: Lloyd Albright, pastor of Emanuel Congregation; his wife, Trudy, assistant principal at Evans Elementary School; their sons, Ian, age six, and Jared, age eight.

LUKE AVALON: A member of Emanuel and chair of the youth committee.

HAL BECKMAN: A member of the Emanuel Disaster Prepare and Respond Team (DPR); coordinator of the congregation's virtual community communications system; and communications coordinator at Green County Hospital.

GINNY CAMPBELL: An Emanuel member and a volunteer at the Red Cross shelter hosted by the congregation.

Disaster Prepare and Response Team: Abbreviated as DPR; Emanuel's response team.

Sammy Ellison: An Emanuel member; a local emergency medical technician (EMT) volunteer; employee of a local hardware store; a member of the DPR team.

Rick Fenner: A pastor from out of town who comes to help with the recovery effort and returns to stay for three months to help Emanuel and Pastor Albright.

Fred Gleason: Member of Emanuel and chair of the property committee.

Clarence Goodyear: Head of the Emanuel's judicatory district and the denominational regional representative to support the congregation through the recovery process.

Eric Gulian: Mayor of Caldwell.

Jill Hanson: Team leader of the Emanuel Disaster Prepare and Respond team.

Cindy Henderson: A recently retired teacher and a member of the Emanuel DPR team.

Irene Hunter: An Emanuel member who lives in a Caldwell retirement community; leader of the volunteer group that folds church bulletins and newsletters.

Gene Johnson: Emanuel property manager, a paid staff member.

Monica Latrell: Director of the Emanuel preschool program, a member of the congregation, and member of one of the Caldwell families whose home was flooded.

Clara Longstreth: An eighty-seven-year-old survivor of the disaster and a volunteer in the recovery process.

Jackie Lorenski: A retired out-of-state social worker with childhood ties to Caldwell. She comes out of retirement to work for a national faith-based disaster-response agency.

Peg Mitchell: An Emanuel congregation member with a large capacity for compassion and a low tolerance for patience and working through existing structures.

FAITH MONROE: A member of the DPR team who coordinates a Red Cross shelter in the early days of the recovery and volunteers in other capacities later in the process. She is a veteran of several floods in other places.

DENNIS PRANDLE: A Caldwell police officer.

LACY ROGERS: A member of Emanuel and chair of the finance committee.

DANA SCOFIELD: A paid staff member of a national faith-based disaster response organization, whose job is coordination of a Camp Comeback day-camp program.

JACK SHAFFER: A paid voluntary agency liaison (VAL) for the Federal Emergency Management Agency (FEMA).

JOHN SULLIVAN: An Emanuel DPR team member and a retired telephone company manager.

CHARLIE TOPLER: A member of Emanuel who is homebound following a stroke; father of two grown children, Julie and Will.

HELEN WILSON: A member of Emanuel and a retired nurse.

SUZANNE WINTERS: Pastor of another Caldwell congregation.

EVELYN WRIGHT: Office administrator at Emanuel, a longtime member of the congregation, and confidant of many Emanuel members.

LILLIAN YEAGER: A regional representative of Emanuel's denominational national disaster response organization.

INTRODUCTION

Get Trained, Get Ready, Get Going

There will be great earthquakes,
famines and pestilences in various places,
and fearful events and great signs from heaven.
—Luke 21:11

When a disaster occurs, we want to know why it happened. Whose fault was it? We can't help asking such questions, even though we can never adequately answer them. Regardless of the nature or cause of a disaster, common elements come into play. After the initial impact, predictable phases of rescue, relief, and recovery follow. A well-organized network of both paid and volunteer professionals begins to appear on the scene, each with a part to play. People react and respond in predictable ways. Life will never "get back to normal." However, gradually, in the months and years to follow, a "new normal" will begin to emerge. Disaster recovery follows a predictable timetable, influenced by such factors as:

- The typical behavior and emotional cycles common in experiences of loss and grief.
- The time required to restore infrastructures to their pre-disaster condition.
- The effectiveness of the leaders who manage the recovery process.

We are all vulnerable to a disaster of some type. We may not be able to avoid one or predict when, where, or how one will disrupt us or our communities. However, we can learn how to prepare for a disaster and how best to respond should we experience one or want to help others who have.

The word disaster derives from a Latin word that means "against the stars." A disaster is typically defined as an event that disrupts normal life, causing physical or mental trauma and/or damage to personal property or community infrastructures such as:

- Random shootings
- Earthquakes
- Forest fires
- Tropical storms and hurricanes
- Windstorms and tornadoes
- Excessive rain that results in flooding and mudslides
- Commercial and industrial accidents, resulting in collisions, collapses, or explosions
- Acts of terrorism, such as bombings, hijackings, or the taking of hostages

This book is an introduction for people of faith who are new to the ministry of disaster preparedness and response. It is impossible to cover in one book all possible types of disasters or all aspects of the recovery process. Nonetheless, professional disaster-response personnel want and depend on volunteers from faith communities to assist in community disaster preparedness and response efforts.

Religious organizations collectively have quick access to thousands of members with a willingness to serve their neighbors. When these volunteers are mobilized, they become a powerful force for good in a time of extreme community distress. The better prepared these volunteers are for disaster-response ministry, the more valuable their presence will be. This book is intended to:

- Give an overview of disaster-response networks already in place to respond to the next disaster that could befall a community.
- Help readers understand the predictable phases of disaster recovery at both the individual and community level.
- Lift up helpful and unhelpful ways that congregational leaders and members can be involved in disaster-response efforts.
- Provide resources to prepare you and your congregation to respond appropriately should a disaster happen in your community.

Although we cannot predict most disasters, there are nonetheless good reasons to prepare for a disaster:

- Disaster preparation and training can bring people together and help them remain calm in the face of disaster.
- A trained group of individuals is a valuable asset to disaster-recovery efforts.
- Developing a disaster-response plan for a congregation can make other types of large-group planning easier.
- Getting involved in disaster preparedness introduces congregation members to a broader disaster-response community network. This acquaintance makes it easier for members to get involved when a disaster occurs and helps identify the congregation as a "team player" that others can count on in a time of need.

To help us fulfill these goals, we have created a fictional disaster in a fictional location. Since many types of disaster include flooding, we've based the fictional disaster on a flood. Each chapter will include:

- A timeline to show the reader at what point in the unfolding disaster the situation discussed in the chapter takes place.

- A description of the current situation.
- A decision facing the fictional congregation's leadership.
- Information that disaster-response volunteers and congregations need to know about some aspect of disaster-response ministry.
- Issues for your local congregation to consider as you determine how and to what extent to get involved.

Throughout the fictional disaster account, the reader will find supplemental information about disaster preparedness and response. Most of this information is based on interviews with disaster-response professionals such as staff of FEMA (the Federal Emergency Management Administration), the Red Cross, and national faith-based disaster-response organizations. The appendixes provide checklists, resources to help you do your own disaster-preparedness work, and additional helpful information. Also included throughout the book are suggestions for further reading, resources for training volunteers, and contact information for organizations active in disaster preparedness and response work.

Unless otherwise identified, the people in this book are fictional. However, their situations and stories are based on real people and events. The authors have chosen to create a fictional narrative to describe the reactions of actual people to protect the privacy of the men, women, and children whose lives have been forever changed by the impact of the disasters they experienced.

CHAPTER 1

The Calm before the Storm

BEFORE DISASTER STRIKES

We know that the whole creation has been groaning as in the pains of childbirth right up to the present time.
—Romans 8:22

Timeline

The members of Emanuel Church are about to experience their first disaster since developing the congregation's Prepare and Respond Plan. The disaster will demonstrate that the effort was needed and will test the effectiveness of the plan.

Situation

It was Wednesday morning on an overcast early September day in Caldwell, a community of about thirty-five thousand located southwest of Yorkshire, a midwestern metropolitan area of nearly a million people. When the alarm went off at 6:30 A.M., Pastor Lloyd Albright stretched and mentally reviewed the day's "to-do" list. After his wife, Trudy, left for work at Evans Elementary School, he completed his morning routines. He then switched on the morning TV news and started rounding up the things he'd need in the office.

The "crawl" across the bottom of the TV screen warned of high winds with driving rains. It looked as if Yorkshire was going to get the worst of a nasty storm, and Emanuel was only sixty-five miles southwest of the city. All too often, flooding followed such storms in the region.

Lloyd forgot about his plans for the day and began wondering whether he should activate the disaster plans he and the six-member Emanuel Disaster Prepare and Respond (DPR) team had spent a year putting together. What should he do first? Call Trudy, who was by now already an hour into her day as assistant principal? Call Jill Hanson, Emanuel's DPR team captain? Call ever-reliable Evelyn, the administrator who had probably arrived at the church office at least an hour ago? His decision was made for him: the phone rang.

"Pastor, we've got a problem." It was Gene, the church property manager. "Evelyn just talked to me. Monica called to say she heard there's going to be massive flooding in our area, and she doesn't think it's safe to open the school today. What do you think we should do?" Monica Latrell had directed Emanuel's preschool for five years, and people had come to rely on her good judgment.

"How hard is it raining there?" the pastor asked. Although the Albrights lived only five miles from the church, sometimes it rained at the church but not in their neighborhood.

"Some. It's not bad yet."

Lloyd replied, "I'll be in as soon as I can. Call Monica back and tell her not to come in. Ask her to activate the parents' phone and e-mail tree. Please put up the "School Closed Due to Bad Weather" sign. Then, would you please pull up the website weather reports for me so I can get in the car and head over? Try to get a reading on where this storm is and what we can expect."

The rain fell harder as Lloyd drove toward Emanuel. A news alert on the radio caught his attention. "We interrupt this program to bring you this urgent news bulletin from the National Weather Service. Water levels in the Green River are rising rapidly. County engineers warn that there could be a breach in the levees in Green County." That stunning news was repeated a few more times before the announcer added that Mayor Eric Gulian was meeting with public-safety officials to decide whether an evacuation was necessary. "Residents along State Route 49 who live within five miles of the Green River are advised that they may be asked to evacuate," he said.

Lloyd said a quick prayer of thanksgiving that only a few of his parishioners lived in the potential evacuation zone. Most members lived west or north of town—away from the Green River. Emanuel was located near Route 49, north of the Caldwell town square. If people living south or east of town had to evacuate, they'd be passing within a couple of blocks of the church. Quite a few members worked in the central Caldwell business district, and although it was outside the flood plain, Lloyd was aware of other communities that had seen floods in areas that had never before flooded. He worried that it might happen here this time and wondered how Emanuel could best respond.

The Emanuel DPR team had suggested that the church become a shelter. The church council had not yet approved the recommendation though, wanting to study the likely impact on the facilities. Nor had the congregation yet been through the Red Cross congregational shelter training program. Two of the DPR team members had taken the Red Cross Volunteer orientation on their own. One factor in the decision to open a shelter was the Red Cross policy that the congregation would have to train enough volunteers to have two or more people at the shelter around the clock. It was a big commitment. Team members Faith Monroe and Sammy Ellison wanted to be prepared to work in another shelter if Emanuel never opened its facilities as a shelter. Faith had done some volunteer work with the Red Cross in Ohio before moving to Caldwell. As an emergency medical technician (EMT), Sammy had delivered people to Red Cross shelters, but had never volunteered in one.

Putting the DPR plan together had been a long and challenging project. Some church members thought it an inappropriate use of time and energy. Team members often heard comments like "That's the government's job. That's why we pay taxes." Or "Doesn't the Red

Cross take care of that?" or "We have enough to do managing our own households. We don't have time to mess with disaster plans for our congregation."

But thanks to patient and persistent leadership within the congregation and coaching from the local disaster-response providers, this dedicated team of six had crafted a comprehensive, yet relatively short summary of what they would need to do for each of two plans. Plan A outlined the steps to follow should the disaster cause damage to Emanuel's buildings or to the homes of members. Plan B laid out the steps the team would follow if the disaster happened within their county or state but not in their own community.

"Now the rubber hits the road," Lloyd thought as he pulled into his parking spot. He dashed through the rain to the canopy over the entrance to the office wing of Emanuel's sprawling facility. He remembered how excited he'd been when he was asked to consider taking the post of senior pastor here. Now, as he worried about the cost of repairing the facilities, he sometimes wondered if a little rural congregation wouldn't have been easier to manage. The structure included a fellowship area, an extensive education area that served as a preschool during the week and a gathering space for more than 250 people of all ages on weekends, two worship spaces, a commercial kitchen, and a large youth wing. Something always needed attention. Most of the facilities were old and in need of major repairs. Also, the growing numbers of young families were hoping the congregation would add on a recreation center.

As soon as he walked in, Evelyn flagged him down with an urgent message from the local Red Cross chapter. "They want to know if we'll open as a shelter. They're afraid their usual facilities might be flooded or unable to handle the numbers of people evacuating. I told them we haven't completed the shelter training yet and our council hasn't voted on the matter. But they're really concerned that their existing shelters will overflow. She said their evaluation of our facilities ranked us as one of the better options right now. What should I tell them?"

The Red Cross was predicting unusually high numbers of evacuations even though the Green River Valley had not flooded in modern times. Local people still told stories about the flood of 1926 that took place two counties over. They were also aware of the massive flooding in the Grand Forks, North Dakota, area in the late 1990s. The memory of these events had people on edge. Many who weren't asked to evacuate were already packing their belongings and heading for higher ground, wherever they could find a motel room or a friend or relative with an available guest room.

Already things were starting to change: many area employers were encouraging people to stay home in case they needed to prepare their property and their families for potential flooding. Lloyd took advantage of this situation by calling the DPR team for an emergency lunch meeting. He offered up another prayer of gratitude for the team they'd pulled together. It included himself; Jill Hanson, a paralegal at a medium-size firm in Yorkshire; Faith Monroe, a nurse in a local general-practice medical clinic; Hal Beckman, a new member who had relocated to be near family when his home and the hospital where he worked in New Orleans were destroyed when the levees were breached after Hurricane Katrina; Sammy Ellison, a long-time EMT volunteer on his days off from managing the local hardware store; Cindy Henderson, a retired middle-school teacher, recently widowed and in search of a cause; and John Sullivan, a former phone company manager retired after thirty-five years with the company.

What a blessing to work with such competent, calm, responsive people! All six reported back within minutes that they would attend the meeting. While Lloyd was talking with the team members, Evelyn called the Red Cross office to say they'd make a decision after lunch.

As the team gathered, Lloyd realized how frazzled he felt already. Although the planning team had prepared for just such an event, now that a potential disaster was unfolding, he and the others weren't so confident about how best to respond. The entire team had taken the county emergency management training, along with fifteen others from Emanuel. They'd published the address of the website for the FEMA online training program in every monthly newsletter to help parishioners be prepared. However, without the Red Cross orientation and without the congregation's having had a chance to approve such a use for the facilities, Lloyd felt unnerved at such a commitment. What would they be committing to? Who would be using their building? Would guests be respectful of the property? Would Emanuel be able to come up with enough volunteers?

Lloyd was about to suggest that maybe they weren't ready when Faith Monroe spoke: "I know it's a risk, but I think we just have to do this. Green County is a lot like the communities along the Ohio River where I used to live. If there is flooding, the people who have the fewest options will be in the most danger. I think we need to do this."

Sammy chimed in next: "I'm all for helping folks. That's what I do on my days off. But I've got to tell you—some of the people we're likely to have aren't exactly your 'go-to-church' types. They'll want to smoke. They'll want to drink. They'll get restless and bored. I don't feel right about doing this without at least the backing of the council."

Lloyd felt a heaviness come over him as he offered his opinion. "I don't see that we have that option right now. There's no time to call the council together. Let's do this. Let me go back to the office and get an update on the evacuation. If the city or county officials aren't ordering mandatory evacuations, then maybe we can offer to help the Red Cross in a day or two."

A Decision to Make

Should Emanuel open its building as a Red Cross shelter? In a typical situation, about a third of the population resists planning for a disaster. These people believe making preparations means focusing on the negative and catering to people's fears. They also worry that to prepare for a disaster is to court danger—a self-fulfilling prophecy. Yet according to Earl E. Johnson, *preparing* for a disaster is one important step in *responding* to a disaster. Johnson, coordinator of the Spiritual Response Team for the Red Cross, has responded to a variety of disasters in many geographical areas. He teaches that people feel more in control when they have a plan and know what they want to do. People who are prepared are less likely to have to depend on strangers to rescue them.

While some disasters are totally unpredictable, many weather-related disasters are predicted far enough in advance that people have time to prepare. Shelter before, during, and after a disaster-level storm is one major issue congregations and families alike can discuss in advance.

For individuals the issue is whether to "shelter in place" or to evacuate. For congregations the issue may be to protect people caught at the facility during a threatening or dangerous storm. More likely the decision will be whether to open the church as a shelter. That is the decision facing Emanuel on the verge of a community evacuation. Although it is important and helpful to have a disaster preparedness and response plan in place, disasters almost always bring chaos and needs no one thought about ahead of time. A twist on the Boy Scout motto of "Be prepared" is "Prepare for the worst, hope for the best," and it applies double to disaster work.

Subsequent chapters of the story and the appendixes address more issues congregations need to consider. Among the choices before staff and volunteers at Emanuel Church, however, is this one: Do we open our facilities as a shelter? Often there are no right or wrong answers to decisions that have to be made, but several factors to consider. Each congregation must evaluate its situation and make the best decision for its circumstances.

Emanuel has three choices about using its facilities as a shelter: yes, no, and maybe:

Yes, we are willing to open our building as a shelter. What needs to happen next?

- We've spent a year preparing, we think we're ready, and the majority of our people believe this is a part of our ministry to reach out to the community.
- We have a good base of people ready and available to help.
- Our facilities are adequate.
- We know that the Red Cross has a long history of providing emergency shelter, and we are willing to work with that organization.

No, this task is beyond our capability at this time. We'll find other ways to help.

- This job is more than we can handle.
- We do not have adequate volunteer support for the long haul.
- Our kitchen is inadequate to provide three meals a day.
- Our key leadership is opposed and feels strongly that this venture would disrupt ongoing ministries in the congregation.
- Some members are concerned about mixing the shelter population with our preschool children.

Maybe, but we want to do this on our own rather than through official structures.

- We want to reach out to the community, but we are concerned about the limits the Red Cross might impose on us, especially about when and how we could share our faith with shelter residents.

- We want more discretion in screening shelter residents.
- We want to determine the length of time we will remain open.
- We want more say in how we manage the meals we provide and the sleeping arrangements for married couples. Red Cross policy requires separate sleeping areas for men and women, including married couples. (See item 5 on page 14.)

What You Need to Know about . . .

DISASTER SHELTERS

Often our first reaction to a pending disaster at a congregational level is to think about turning the building into a temporary shelter. It seems a logical response to a community need. "People need a safe place to be, and we have space"—that's the thinking of many faithful people. It seems appropriate to welcome the neighbor and stranger in times of need. It makes sense to use space that may be unoccupied many hours a day during the week. When the space is used, it is often for meetings and programs that are likely to be postponed or cancelled anyway, depending on the nature of the disaster. Larger congregations often have buildings well suited for use as shelters. They can provide office equipment, kitchens designed to feed large crowds, classroom space to afford some privacy and quiet time, and restrooms, sometimes even with showers.

Providing shelter may well be an appropriate congregational response to a disaster. However, before making such a decision, leaders need to know some facts about providing shelter:

1. The American Red Cross is the lead agency for the U.S. government, in its National Response Framework, to provide for mass care. The Red Cross also often provides food, emergency medical care, and emotional and spiritual comfort. The

organization frequently uses local congregations to provide these resources.

2. Before a congregation can open a Red Cross shelter in its building, it must form a committee of volunteers who will be trained; the facilities must meet certain standards; and the congregation should be able to staff the shelter with volunteers twenty-four hours a day.
3. Congregations that work with Red Cross are covered under insurance policies of the American Red Cross. Congregations that open on their own need to be prepared to handle any liability that results from hosting shelter guests.
4. The Red Cross will provide cots or mattresses and some means of procuring food to feed residents.
5. The Red Cross policy of separate sleeping arrangements for men and women will have to be addressed on a case-by-case basis when minors come to a shelter with a single parent of the opposite sex. Red Cross staff will assist congregations in working out the details.
6. People who use shelters often do so as a last resort. They may not be pleased about needing to stay in a shelter. They may not have the emotional energy to monitor the behavior of their children, who will likely be upset about the sudden change in family routines.
7. People come to shelters with a variety of needs. Though Red Cross workers screen people before sending them to a shelter, they do not give a local congregation the option of declining potential residents.
8. When a worship center becomes a shelter, it is home to the residents for several days. It will be difficult at best to conduct other programs or ministries as long as the shelter is open.

For more details on the American Red Cross and its response in times of disaster, see appendix A.

Implications for Your Congregation

- Part of your congregation's disaster preparation should include compiling a list of your most vulnerable members, along with contact information for family members to contact on their behalf. The list might include single parents with young children, vulnerable older members who live alone, members with special needs (such as limited mobility, use of oxygen or specialized medical equipment, mental illness), and members recuperating from recent surgery or physical injuries. Speak in advance with these members about where they could go if they needed to evacuate from their homes. Develop a plan to check in with them in advance of a pending disaster and after any major incident that could cause them harm. Many communities now register people with "special needs" in advance of a disaster so that arrangements can be made to transport these people in an evacuation.
- Some congregations offer shelter to their own members who need or want to evacuate or fear to stay home alone through a disaster-size storm. Think about what resources you'd need to accommodate these members. How would they handle bedding, food, and entertainment? One Houston congregation hosted a "family lock-in" when a hurricane threatened the city. Members passed the hours baking cookies, drinking hot chocolate, and learning some of their children's favorite games in the youth room. People brought their own sleeping bags and camped out with one family per Sunday-school room.
- Out of compassion and a sense of call to serve their neighbors, congregations sometimes decide on their own initiative to open their building as a shelter. Before you do this, consider how you will supply bedding, showers and laundry facilities, food service, supervision of children, and the social services that shelter guests will likely require. You should also contact

your insurance carrier to check for limits to your liability coverage if you use your facilities as a shelter.
- The American Red Cross has been operating shelters in schools and churches for decades. If your congregation is interested in becoming one of its sites, the starting place is to invite a staff person from your local chapter to visit with leaders of the congregation.
- Your congregation can support other shelter sites in town without itself hosting a shelter. Again, contact your Red Cross chapter to find out how members of your congregation can support shelter efforts.
- Take stock of your congregation's ability to offer shelter. Do you have adequate space for children to play? Separate sleeping arrangements for women and men? Adequate kitchen facilities to feed people three meals a day? Quiet places for people to get a break from the constant noise that goes with large groups? Shower facilities? Laundry facilities? Access to public transportation? Places for people to make phone calls? Sufficient volunteers to staff the shelter?
- Take stock of the support of members. Hosting a shelter will probably disrupt many aspects of congregational life. Your members will need a safe place to gather and talk about their experiences in the disaster. Will opening the building as a shelter limit how well you can serve your own people?

Resources

Red Cross, *www.redcross.org*

United States Department of Homeland Security, *www.ready.gov*. Resources to help communities and private citizens prepare for a disaster.

New York Disaster Interfaith Services, *www.nydis.org*. Resources to help communities and private citizens prepare for a disaster.

Questions for Reflection

1. If you've ever spent one or more nights in a group shelter, describe that experience. If you haven't, what do you think it would be like?
2. Have you ever been stranded for the night because of weather or other circumstances beyond your control? How did you handle the situation?
3. Have you ever hosted total strangers in your home? If so, what was it like? If not, would you consider doing so? Why or why not?
4. Have you ever been a guest in the home of a total stranger? If so, describe the experience. If not, what do you think it would be like?
5. What would you need to have with you if you had to leave your home and couldn't return for many days or weeks?
6. Can you create a safe place to keep copies of critical items such as birth and marriage certificates, insurance policies, titles to cars and property? You might need to grab these in a hurry in the event of a disaster.
7. What would be your best options for a safe place to go if you had to leave your home?
8. Who needs to know how to reach you at all times? Do these individuals have the contact information they need to do so?

Scripture Reflection

When a stranger sojourns with you in your land, you shall not do him wrong. The stranger who sojourns with you shall be to you as the native among you, and you shall love him as yourself; for you were strangers in the land of Egypt: I am the LORD your God.

—Leviticus 19:33–34 RSV

CHAPTER 2

Hunker Down or Get Out of Town

WHEN DISASTER IS IMMINENT

The LORD is my strength and my song;
he has become my salvation.
—Psalm 118:14

Timeline

It's 8:30 Wednesday night. The disaster is unfolding, and emergency rescue operations will soon be underway. Once evacuations became mandatory, Emanuel's DPR team members felt that they had to respond. They decided to open the church facilities as a Red Cross shelter.

Situation

The rest of Wednesday was filled with calls and e-mails, accompanied by nonstop media coverage of the rising river, record-breaking rainfall, and concern about hurricane-force winds possibly moving in from the Gulf Coast. Many volunteers spent the afternoon at the church moving furniture out of the way as Red Cross workers began converting the fellowship hall into a combination registration area, community gathering room, and dining hall. Other volunteers were setting up cots in the education wing—four or six to a room, men and boys on one floor and women and girls on another. Meanwhile, the storm continued to dump record amounts of rain into the already swollen Green River basin. Citizens had been urged to evacuate, and thousands were trying to do just that. TV news channels were already reporting unusually high volumes of traffic.

Just as Lloyd Albright was about to sit down to the no-longer-warm dinner someone had brought him an hour earlier, his cell phone rang. "Hello, Monica. How are you holding up?" Monica and her family had recently moved into their dream home, which was built into a hill—a two-story house with a half-basement, located just outside the mandatory evacuation area.

"We're OK here for the moment. We've moved to the second floor just in case. My husband is trying to get the kids calmed down enough to sleep. They aren't really scared—just too keyed up with all the excitement around here."

"Well, that's good news. I could use some of that."

"I hate to add to whatever other bad news you've had, but two of my teachers and their families are caught in that traffic mess on Route 49. A third teacher just checked in too. She and her husband are sandbagging their basement walk-out doors. One of the families on Route 49 said they're about out of gas. There are long lines at the gas stations that are hardly moving. If they can make it to Emanuel, would anyone there have gas to give them?

"I don't know. I'm not sure we thought of that one when we put the plan together. I'll get someone to make some calls and get back to you. Are you going to sit tight?"

"Absolutely. We're high and dry here. Besides, we made our family emergency kit at the workshop—remember?"

Lloyd did remember. Although turnout had been low, the families who came to the "Are You Ready?" event last summer had paid attention and taken steps to prepare themselves and their families.

"OK," he said. "Someone will call you, but I can't promise who or when."

Lloyd called Trudy to say he wouldn't be home any time soon. Trudy said everything was under control on the home front and encouraged him to eat something and try to get some rest in his office. "The news says they're sandbagging the levee along the river. This looks pretty bad. Maybe you ought to stay there tonight?"

Though she said all was well at home, Lloyd thought she sounded nervous and tired. He felt torn between staying at the church and going home. "I don't want to leave you and the boys on your own. I'll try to come home soon." He promised to call her if anything changed. Meanwhile, he had more people to call.

As part of Emanuel's DPR plan, the team had set up virtual communities within the congregation. Each virtual community—VCs, as the team had started calling them—had a community coordinator and assistant coordinator. The plan was that in an emergency, these two would try to call every household in their virtual community to assess how people were doing and if they needed help. Each team was responsible for an average of ten households. Team members had three basic questions to ask anyone they reached in the household over age fifteen:

1. "Is your family safe and doing OK?"
2. "Are you staying or leaving, and if you're leaving, how can we reach you?"
3. Depending on how the first two questions were answered, either, "What do you need at this time?" or "Can anyone in your household volunteer to help with our response efforts?"

Not knowing what situations they might be dealing with, the trained volunteers had learned to focus mostly on active listening skills. They would help reassure any members who seemed unduly concerned or frightened. The team had worked up a simple form to collect information about how to try to reach members of each household if they left town after a disaster. The data-collection sheet also contained names and phone numbers to be given to the Red Cross, emergency services, and the DPR team members for volunteers to have available as a reference.

The DPR team was particularly concerned about a few members who lived alone with no family nearby. Team members were working on lining up a buddy system for each of these people, but they didn't have this part of the plan completed yet. So far, most of their work had focused on determining what they needed to do to prepare the church building for a disaster. They had already backed up critical computer data and arranged to store it at the regional judicatory office. They had a list of people who might need extra help. They were starting to stockpile canned goods in a storage closet. They had rounded up contact information for the DPR team and council members, including everyone's "in case of emergency," or "ICE," numbers.

At lunch earlier that day the DPR team set up a conference call for noon Thursday to establish some consistent way to check in with each other. Of course, they realized they could not know what the next twenty-four hours would bring.

Faith Monroe, an Emanuel volunteer helping get the Red Cross shelter open, said she had heard that more than fifty Caldwell citizens were at work putting sandbags along the river levee—in a torrential downpour. It looked as though it was going to be a long, wet, nail-biting kind of evening.

A few hours ago Lloyd had called Hal Beckman, coordinator of the virtual community team coordinators. Lloyd had asked Hal to launch the "Operation VC Check-in." That was at 4:30 P.M. It was now 8:30, and Lloyd hadn't heard back from Hal or any of the other captains. So he called Hal again.

"Hal, any information I need to know about?"

"I'm sorry I haven't gotten back to you already, Pastor, but I'm not hearing from many of our VC captains. The few I'm hearing from are having trouble reaching any of their VCs. I thought I should keep trying before I got back to you."

"Well, OK. Thanks. Listen, Monica just called. Two of her teachers are evacuating. Another one is sandbagging her basement walkout door. The Swenson family is about out of gas and afraid of the long lines at the gas stations along the way. It's taken them an hour to move three miles, but they still want to try to get to Cal's brother's home in Yorkshire. If they can get to the church, do you think we can find someone who isn't evacuating who could bring some gas? Can you call Monica to find out more details and see if we can help these folks?"

"I'll make a few calls. I know a few people who filled gas cans for their generators. I knew traffic would be bad—but I've never seen it like this! I can see it from the top floor of the hospital. It really is a mess out there." Hal hung up and started scrolling through his cell-phone directory for names to call. He was grateful to have something to do after all the sitting and waiting around for phone calls and e-mails. Normally he would have left the hospital two hours earlier, but since he was considered "essential personnel," he wouldn't be going home any time soon.

Lloyd wasn't the only person still at the church, though. Cindy Henderson sat at the receptionist's desk outside his office. She was one of the volunteers trained by Evelyn, the office manager, to help staff the phones in an emergency. That part of the plan was working well. Evelyn made one phone call to the office back-up coordinator. By the close of Evelyn's exhausting day, helpers were scheduled to come in for three-hour shifts to cover the phones. Normally the church office closed at 4:30, but Cindy offered to stay through the evening. "Operation Call Emanuel" was launched and working.

There really wasn't much the church could do for people at this stage, but the volunteers had received a quick orientation about how to respond to anxious callers. Mostly they were there to offer an encouraging word and help people review their plans for evacuating or staying put. Having a person answer the church phone and offer as much up-to-date information as possible did seem to comfort people. Some calls were not urgent. The storm was still raging at full force, but already some people wanted to know if church services would be held Sunday. The volunteers told them to call back Friday; it was too early to know what Sunday would bring.

Other people, especially older and longtime members, called the church for reassurance. News of the rising level of the Green River, combined with reports of seventy-mile-an-hour winds moving into the region, had folks jittery. Even if callers didn't know the volunteer who answered, they felt better talking to a live person after listening to news reporters dispensing frightening news hour after hour. A couple of callers said how grateful they were to know the shelter was there—"just in case," although it was unlikely any members of Emanuel would end up using it.

Lloyd was two bites into the dinner he no longer wanted when Cindy came into his office. "Pastor, I'm sorry to interrupt your dinner, but you need to know about this one."

"It's OK, Cindy. What's up?"

"It's Charlie Topler's daughter, Julie. Charlie's home alone and probably scared to death, but he won't admit it. His son, Will, stayed with him until after lunch, and Julie was supposed to be there hours ago to spend the rest of the day. They all thought Charlie would be alone for only an hour, and Charlie insisted he'd be OK watching a movie while he waited. But Julie's been stuck in the traffic jam on Route 49 for five hours and has only gotten halfway there—she still has ten miles to go. She's called Charlie a couple of times, and Charlie told Julie he heard a huge cracking sound out behind the house, but he can't get his wheelchair back there to see what happened."

Charlie, an eighty-four-year-old veteran, had had a minor stroke the previous spring. His two adult children, who both mercifully lived within an hour's drive of his home, had persuaded Charlie's doctor not to release him from rehab until Charlie reluctantly agreed to have someone with him at all times for the next six months. So far, Julie and Will and members of their families had been able to provide the support they thought he needed. But the storm and evacuation had disrupted their daily schedule. Julie had decided to call Emanuel after she figured out that Charlie hadn't revealed any of this information to his VC coordinator.

Lloyd's first inclination was to go over to Charlie's house himself and bring him to the church, but it occurred to him that he didn't even know whether the roads into Charlie's neighborhood would be passable. He also realized that he wouldn't be able to get Charlie's wheelchair into his own car and that perhaps he really didn't know how to adequately handle someone recovering from a stroke. In all his recent visits to Charlie someone from Charlie's family had handled his personal needs. Lloyd went simply to offer pastoral care.

A Decision to Make

Should Pastor Albright rescue Charlie himself? Although the Emanuel DPR team had tried to think through all possible scenarios, disasters by their nature include challenges that no one can predict. People who are drawn into ministry and volunteer work often feel compelled to respond immediately to another's need. Their capacity to care sometimes motivates them to do whatever is needed to assist others. While this trait benefits many people, it can be a challenge in a disaster. The adrenaline tends to run high; in combination with pressing needs, it can cloud a person's thinking. One may act more impulsively than usual and make unwise decisions. People used to caring for others may have unrealistic expectations about their own energy or how much they can accomplish.

As the designated spiritual leader of Emanuel, Lloyd needs to consider his options carefully. It is true that Charlie needs help right now and would no doubt trust Lloyd. However, many others look to Lloyd for leadership and a calm presence. That list includes Trudy and the boys.

One benefit of disaster-preparedness planning is that it helps clarify critical roles for community members. Some may think that they aren't doing enough after a disaster. Regardless of how many hours they put in or how many people they help, still more people are in need of assistance. A disaster-preparation plan helps to establish priorities for leaders and to set reasonable expectations for how much any one team member can do.

Again, there are often no right or wrong answers when decisions need to be made. Nonetheless, Lloyd must decide how best to respond to Charlie's situation. Should he go get Charlie?

Yes, Pastor Albright remains convinced that it is his responsibility to take care of Charlie, a member of his congregation.

- Charlie trusts him and will come with him but might not be willing to leave his home with someone else.
- The wheelchair will be a challenge, but Lloyd knows he can borrow an SUV from someone at the church.
- Lloyd assumes one of the many volunteers at the church will be able to tend to whatever needs Charlie may have.
- Charlie's son and daughter will feel much less anxious if they know their father is safe and sound at Emanuel.
- Cindy would probably be willing to stay to cover phones at the church while the pastor goes to get Charlie. He could retrieve messages from his cell phone later.

No, Pastor Albright is not trained to serve as search-and-rescue personnel. Trained rescue workers would be better equipped to help Charlie.

- Lloyd's responsibility is either to report Charlie's situation to the rescue authorities or to delegate that job to an Emanuel DPR team member.
- He could try to call Julie or Will and give one of them information about how to report their father's situation to emergency rescue officials.
- Emanuel DPR team members previously thought about what to do in such a situation. They had agreed that Lloyd should stay either at home or at the church, where people could reach him—unless, of course, he needed to evacuate with his family for their safety. One challenge of disaster-preparedness work

is not knowing what the situation will be and yet needing to prepare for it. In the intensity of the moment, Lloyd forgot the team's discussion and decision.

Rescue: The First Stage of Disaster Response

SAR (search and rescue) teams are trained and dispatched by local and regional governmental entities such as the U.S. Coast Guard and National Guard. USAR (urban search and rescue) teams operate the same way but have special training to work in urban areas where an earthquake or explosion could cause massive damage to infrastructure. These teams undergo extensive training and drills. They have access to life-saving equipment—boats for flooded areas and helicopters for airlifts, for example.

Maybe. Lloyd is deeply concerned about Charlie's situation.

- However, he is also aware of how many other people look to him for comfort and calm in a chaotic situation.
- He could try to identify someone else to handle Charlie's situation. Emanuel has a team of caregivers trained to visit shut-ins and people dealing with illness, a death in the family, or another crisis. Maybe one of them could stay with Charlie until Julie or a rescue worker arrives.
- If he is unable to find someone else to go, he can go himself and recruit another member of Emanuel's DPR team to take calls at the church.

What You Need to Know about . . .

EVACUATIONS

Communities have their own ways of handling evacuations. Once local officials deem the public to be in a potentially dangerous situation, it is the responsibility of the mayor, sheriff, county judge, or other government official to call for an evacuation, either voluntary or mandatory. Even in a mandatory evacuation, some people will refuse to leave. Generally local and regional government officials do not have the authority to physically remove a person from his or her home. Their primary focus is to strongly encourage residents to leave potentially dangerous situations.

In general, it's up to the local officials to call on their state for help if a situation is too severe to handle with local resources. It is then up to state officials to call on the federal government for assistance. Typically this process happens within hours—primarily via conference calls. When the pending disaster can be predicted—when a hurricane, flood, or wildfire is approaching—government disaster-management officials begin coordinating evacuation, rescue, and relief efforts well in advance. Rescue and relief teams are put on alert and begin moving toward the area, ready to move in as soon as requested. By declaring an event to be a federal disaster, the U.S. government opens up access to a variety of resources. Chapter 7 deals with this topic in more detail.

Under what circumstances do officials call for an evacuation? How do individual heads of households decide whether to stay or go? One factor is the intensity of the disaster. If at all possible, officials would prefer that people "shelter in place" to keep freeways and other routes open for emergency-response efforts.

Shelter in Place?

As in any vocation, people who work in disaster preparedness and response work have developed their own "insider" language. "Shelter in place" is a term officials use when people face a potentially dangerous situation and officials want them to secure their homes and stay put. Local media generally provide details about preparing to shelter in place or evacuate. It is up to each household and congregation to secure property and protect people.

However, in severe conditions such as threat of hurricane-force winds, out-of-control forest fires, or danger of flooding, officials want to get everyone out of the area as quickly as possible to reduce the number of casualties and to make rescue efforts easier. How many people need to evacuate varies greatly from event to event. A hurricane could result in evacuating millions of people, as residents of urban areas along the coast are advised to leave. A river flooding in a rural area may require evacuating only those people living within a few miles on either side of the river. The general natural-disaster wisdom says, “Run from the water; hide from the wind.” In other words, if there is danger of flooding, get out. If high winds are headed your way, stay where you are if you are in a sturdy, substantial structure.

It takes many hours and a large commitment of staff and resources to organize for the mass evacuation of a large population area. People need to be prepared for shortages of gasoline, water, and food along evacuation routes. If the power goes out, so do gas-station pumps and ATMs. Cash becomes superior to other methods of payment. People who live in areas where evacuation orders are a predictable fact of life need to keep enough cash on hand to cover the expenses of an evacuation. Government officials vary in their judgment of when to call for an evacuation. “Getting out” is an enormous inconvenience to everyone concerned, and no public official wants to deal with the frustration and public outcry that will follow if the anticipated disaster doesn’t materialize. However, neither does any public servant want to risk endangering lives by failing to call for an evacuation.

Implications for Your Congregation

Kevin Massey, executive director of Lutheran Disaster Response, told a group of clergy that in times of trouble, most people turn first to their religious communities and leaders. Churches will be called on to help in many ways as the post-disaster recovery process unfolds. Church leaders are in a good position to support local emergency-planning efforts by helping their members prepare for a disaster. The more thoroughly citizens are prepared for a disaster, the fewer demands will be made on disaster-response personnel. Congregations can support disaster preparation work in several ways:

1. Congregations can reinforce the messages officials disseminate about how residents can secure property, protect lives, and prepare to be self-sufficient for two to three days.
2. Congregations can host "Are You Ready?" events that help people think about disaster-preparedness issues, assemble family emergency kits, make copies of critical paperwork, and so forth.
3. Congregations can keep a supply of items people might need in an emergency and pass these out as needed to members. These could include basic health and hygiene items, cleaning supplies, and items to entertain children (of all ages!) during the long hours of waiting.
4. Congregations can provide information about emergency-response agencies in the area, literature with prayers and sacred readings from their faith tradition, and emergency-contact information for key leaders of their faith community.

People may be reluctant to evacuate. Congregations may be in a position to help members address their concerns by providing accurate information and helping them make plans that are right for their situation. People resist evacuating for a variety of reasons:

1. They don't want to leave their pets behind. Since Hurricane Katrina, many shelters have changed their polocies regarding pets. See "Get Ready, Get Set, Go" below for details.
2. People don't believe the situation is as serious as news reports suggest and want to avoid the hassle and inconvenience of evacuating.

3. People are afraid of looting or other damage to their property and believe they can do something to protect their property if they stay—and they know that once they leave, they cannot.
4. They love adventure and want to see the action up close.
5. They don't know where to go, fear getting stranded on the road, or don't have enough money to evacuate.

Get Ready, Get Set, Go

See appendix B for suggested items to have ready should you need to evacuate, and supplies to have on hand if you may need to shelter in place.

- *On the road again.* Decide ahead of time where you will go. If your destination is a motel or hotel, take the website address and phone number with you. Make reservations as soon as you decide to go.
- *Travel light.* Take only the essentials that can't be replaced, fill your gas tank, avoid unnecessary trips before you leave, and leave as quickly as possible to reduce your time on the road.
- *Wait your turn.* In urban areas officials may evacuate by zones or zip codes. Everyone benefits from the orderly evacuation of a region, so stay posted for announcements, and wait your turn.
- *Get on the bus.* Larger communities may have buses on call for mass evacuations. Your local government websites and news media are the best starting places to get information about such plans. This knowledge will be especially important for any people in your community with medical, physical, or mental disabilities. In many communities these people can register in advance to help officials better provide for them. Check with your local city or county government for details.
- *Leaving on a jet plane?* If you want to evacuate by plane, make a reservation as soon as possible and pay the extra money for a refundable ticket. In times of disaster the situation

can and most likely will change. Expect delays. Be aware that airports may have to close to preserve the safety of their personnel and equipment.

- *Don't forget your furry friends.* After Hurricane Katrina, the American Red Cross changed its policy on pets in shelters. Pets are now allowed in shelters if they are contained in crates and their shots are up to date. Check the website of the American Humane Society of the United States (*www.hsus.org*), which offers a page of information about care of animals during a disaster, a manual to help communities include animals in their disaster plans, and a quiz to gauge your disaster-preparedness IQ.

Resources

National Hurricane Center, *www.nhc.noaa.gov*

The Weather Underground, *www.wunderground.com*, a website for tracking weather and for accessing other weather information.

Questions for Reflection

1. Have you ever had to leave your home in a hurry because of a fire or other disaster? What did you take with you? What were the hardest things to leave behind?
2. What was the worst storm or other danger you've experienced? How did you handle it? What would you do differently if you were in that situation again?
3. Have you ever been lost, with no idea of where you were or how you'd get out of the situation? What got you through that experience? What advice do you have for others who might find themselves in that situation some day?

4. Describe the biggest traffic jam you've encountered. What caused it? How did you handle it?
5. If you had to leave your home in an emergency, where could you go?
6. Ask family members to tell what items they'd want to take with them if they had to leave in a hurry. Then challenge everyone to think how to fit everything into one vehicle.
7. Who is the first person outside your household that you'd call in an emergency? Do you keep his or her contact information with you at all times?

Scripture Reflection

The LORD lives; and blessed be my rock,
and exalted be the God of my salvation.
—Psalm 18:46 RSV

CHAPTER 3

D-Day and Taking Stock

COMMUNICATIONS IN CHAOTIC CONDITIONS

God is our refuge and strength,
an ever-present help in trouble.
Therefore we will not fear, though the earth gives way
and the mountains fall into the heart of the sea,
though its waters roar and foam
and the mountains quake with their surging.
—Psalm 46:1–3

Timeline

Later Wednesday evening and early Thursday morning. The damage that occurred overnight was more severe than anticipated. In addition to the flooding in never-before-flooded areas, the remains of a Category 3 hurricane that hit the Gulf Coast twenty-six hours earlier battered the community. Overnight, high winds drove rain into crevices of buildings, knocked down trees, and hurled small objects through windows throughout the area. Although the rain ended in the early morning hours, the high winds continued until just before dawn. This is the Disaster D-Day for which the leaders of Emanuel congregation have tried to prepare themselves and their community.

Situation

Sheer exhaustion, if nothing else, had solved Lloyd Albright's dilemma about whether to rescue Charlie himself. When he stood up the previous evening to refill his coffee cup for the six or seventh time, he realized how totally exhausted he was— mentally, physically, and spiritually. He decided he was in no condition to evacuate Charlie; he needed to go home and get some sleep, or he would be no good to anyone.

After telling Faith Monroe in the Red Cross shelter about Charlie's situation, he headed home. Faith had ridden out four floods during her years in Ohio, where she had lived until recently. When she learned that staff and volunteers at Emanuel were considering getting trained so that the church could serve as a Red Cross shelter, she practically pounced on congregational leaders to take that step. She'd served in several shelters during flooding along the Ohio River; she knew that willing congregations with members trained to host shelters were desperately needed. She also knew that the discipline of preparing to qualify Emanuel as a shelter would benefit members in many ways.

Faith was the first to volunteer to stay at Emanuel once the team agreed to open the church as a shelter. Now she counseled Lloyd to call Charlie's daughter, Julie, with the phone numbers of several local rescue operations and to let her focus on her father's situation. "Those who can help should help," she said. It saddened Lloyd to think of the once vibrant and self-sufficient Charlie at home alone and frightened. The stroke had taken its toll on Charlie. The man hated needing help, but it was clear to Lloyd from his visits with Charlie that he would need it now.

"Besides," Faith insisted, "you know Julie's got to be frantic with worry. Giving her something specific to do will help keep her anxiety in check." Faith encouraged Lloyd to go home. "Your family needs you, and you need the break. The storm isn't even over yet. We have a long way to go."

Faith had seen more than her share of dedicated pastors and lay volunteers burn out trying to do it all at the start of a disaster. They rushed in to help with no sense of how long their help would be needed or what their families would sacrifice to support their Good Samaritan intentions. It was part of her unspoken mission to try to keep people from self-destructing by responding too soon with too much of themselves.

Lloyd reluctantly dragged himself home to sleep in his own bed. After unwinding briefly with Trudy and checking on their sleeping sons—six-year-old Ian and eight-year-old Jared—Lloyd fell into bed. He was snoring within five minutes, even with all that caffeine in his system.

Amazingly, the whole Albright family slept through the high winds that blew through the community for three and a half hours starting at 2:00 A.M. The storm wouldn't run out of steam until it crossed the border into Canada over the weekend.

Later Caldwell citizens would learn that communities from Chicago to Cleveland had lost power in the aftermath of the storm. Lloyd and others in the community had been vaguely aware that a large hurricane was heading inland from the Gulf of Mexico, at the same time the Caldwell folk were dealing with the local severe late-summer storms. However, they never anticipated dealing with the aftermath of a hurricane in addition to their local storm.

A Storm by Any Other Label Is Still a Threat

The public tends to use terms interchangeably to talk about storms consisting of high winds and heavy rains. Meteorologists who predict the onslaught of these intense storms use specific criteria to define a hurricane, a tropical storm, or a tropical depression. In the Western Hemisphere these are the common terms for high winds and, sometimes, water surges. People in other parts of the world may refer to such storms as "cyclones" or "typhoons." A "tsunami" is the result of a natural occurrence under the ocean—such as earthquakes, volcanoes, or explosions—that cause a great sea wave that washes inland.

Hurricanes are divided into five categories; a Category 5 is the most damaging. The categories indicate the potential damage, including flooding, when a hurricane makes landfall, although the criteria are not universal. The category number also predicts the height of the water surge at landfall.

Categories for Storms in the Western Hemisphere

CATEGORY	WIND SPEED (in miles per hour)	ANTICIPATED WATER SURGE (in feet)
Category 5	More than 156	More than 18
Category 4	131–155	13–18
Category 3	111–130	9–12
Category 2	96–110	6–8
Category 1	74–95	4–6
Tropical storm	39–73	0–3
Tropical depression	Up to 38	Surges not expected

The History of Naming Hurricanes

Attaching names to major storms that escalate to hurricane strength makes communications quicker and less likely to be misinterpreted than the alternative of using longitude and latitude descriptions. Hundreds of weather stations and ships at sea need to communicate with each other clearly and carefully, particularly when a major storm is developing.

Historically, storms in the West Indies were named for the saint on whose day the storm occurred. An Australian meteorologist started giving tropical storms women's names in the late 1800s. That tradition, adopted also by American meteorologists, ended in 1978 when men's and women's names began to be used alternately for storms. A storm name may be retired from the list of possibilities when the damage or loss of life from the storm of that name is sufficiently devastating.

The overnight winds blew hundreds of large trees into power lines along a several-hundred-mile stretch through the nation's center. Meanwhile, Green County residents' worst fears about the Green River's cresting were also realized. The river had swollen to a two-mile-wide rush of brown, murky water. This overflow, aggravated by hours of unrelenting rain, was now seeping into the basements and first floors of hundreds of homes. While some people were trying to cope with the rising water, others were dealing with water damage from rain coming in through leaking roofs and windows broken by the high winds and torrential rainfall.

Lloyd and Trudy woke up at about 6:00 A.M., completely unaware of the night's events. Since he couldn't see the time on the alarm clock, Lloyd pushed the switch on his bedside table lamp. No light. "Trudy, I think we lost power overnight."

"Great," she muttered, half awake. "Try the phone." Lloyd sat on the side of the bed with the cordless receiver. He sat for several discouraging moments listening to the sound of silence, hoping that if he held the phone long enough he'd be rewarded with a dial tone. "Nothing," he said.

They got up, dressed hastily, and raced outside. A stunning scene greeted them. "Oh, my God," Trudy blurted out as they tried to take in what they saw in the gray early-morning light. The beautiful oak tree, more than a century old, which had been the boys' favorite place to play, now lay across the driveway at a 45-degree angle with its roots sticking up grotesquely. Only their neighbor's garage had kept the felled tree from hitting the ground. Looking around, they realized they had lots of company; the whole neighborhood was littered with downed branches and other debris.

They had prepared for flooding in the region, but they were unprepared for the debris they saw everywhere they looked—put there by the gale-force winds they'd managed to sleep through.

"At least we aren't flooded—yet," Lloyd said.

Trudy stood silently weeping. She felt totally defeated. An unfamiliar heaviness made her feel as though she were being pushed down by a large, invisible hand. She found it difficult to breathe. She felt numb and immobile. She stood transfixed, unable to comprehend the chaotic landscape.

"We have to do something," Lloyd said finally. "We can't just stare at this all day."

"I know," Trudy said without conviction. "But what are we going to do?"

A combination of adrenaline, desperation, and determination began to replace their initial shock. "We'll try to find out what's going on," Lloyd said. They went back into the house and pulled out the disaster prep kit they'd assembled at the "Are You Ready?" event last summer. After a few minutes they were able to get some news on a battery-powered radio. They sat as though in a trance, hearing the first descriptions of what had happened to their peaceful community the night before. They heard the news but couldn't absorb it. It was almost like an out-of-body experience.

All-news stations reported overnight sustained winds of sixty miles per hour for three and a half hours. Reports were also coming in about roads closed by debris and high water. Drinking water was possibly contaminated. People were being warned not to drink it without first boiling it for at least five minutes. Further, they should not attempt to sterilize floodwater.

Electrical power was out for an estimated twenty-five thousand Green Valley Power and Light customers. Thousands more were without power throughout the Midwest. The Green River had overflowed its banks at 4:35 A.M. Newscasters reported massive flooding in the Green River Valley. "Do not attempt to drive through water. Stay in your home if you are not flooded. Leave roads clear for emergency personnel. If you have floodwater in your home, move as high as possible. Find something to use as a flag to notify rescue workers of your location. Stay tuned for further news." The radio announcer repeated the headline reports over and over as Trudy and Lloyd sat stunned.

Lloyd tried his cell phone and discovered that he had no service. Gradually Trudy began to feel desperate to do something—

anything. She wondered if her school was flooded, or if it would be used as a shelter—and if she'd be called upon to help manage things if it was. She felt like a caged animal. She needed to get up and move. But she had no idea where to go or what to do. Everything she thought about doing she could not do. She realized that she couldn't cook breakfast. Or listen to CDs. Or watch TV. Or check e-mail. The boys wouldn't be able to play their video games. With neither cell phones nor their home phone working, they couldn't call anyone, nor could any of their friends and relatives call them—people who would no doubt hear of the flooding and worry about them. It didn't look as though they could even leave until some of the larger trees were cleared from their street. Who knew how long that would take?

"I wonder if the reason our home phone isn't working is because it's a cordless that requires electricity," Lloyd suggested. Trudy remembered they had an old-fashioned pink Princess touch-tone phone in a box in the garage. She'd meant to give it to the local thrift shop but had never gotten around to it. After a little digging through boxes, she found it. "Bingo!" she called out as she plugged it into the wall and immediately heard a dial tone.

"Great!" said Lloyd. "Now, do you suppose anyone we know has an old-fashioned phone that we can call? Maybe this becomes the church office for the next couple of days."

"I'd like that," Trudy said. "I'd really like to have you closer to home until we see what we're up against here. Tears began to overflow and run down her cheeks. Lloyd pulled her close and fought back his own tears. He felt torn. He wanted to be here to hold and comfort Trudy and the boys. Yet he felt compelled to go out into the mess and offer assistance and comfort to the people he served and to their community—if he could even get out. He needed to fulfill his role as a local leader and to use his training in first aid and CPR. The professors forgot to cover this situation in seminary, he thought.

He stood holding Trudy for a long time, trying to pray and discovering he had nothing to say to God at the moment. Surrounded by devastation, Lloyd was also becoming aware of a gnawing doubt in the back of his mind: maybe everything he believed about God might not be true after all. Why do terrible storms destroy lives, and livelihoods and homes? He wasn't sure of anything at the moment: Not his proper role in the midst of dire need. Not his theology of "why bad things happen to good people." Not his publicly professed beliefs about the power of prayer and faith. He felt as though he'd been picked up like Dorothy in *The Wizard of Oz* and dropped off far from home. Everything seemed strange and out of place. He wanted to go home. But he already was home—except that it didn't feel like home right now.

Then he felt guilty for thinking such thoughts while standing in his own kitchen with his family safe, while many others only miles away were losing everything they owned—and maybe their lives or loved ones too. He clung to Trudy with an overwhelming sense of loss and helplessness. He couldn't remember ever feeling at such a loss for some sense of direction. "How can I do any good for anyone else when I can't make sense of this?" he thought. "How am I going to get through this? My God, I don't have any idea what to do or where to start."

Their quiet moments ended abruptly when they heard two equally distracting sounds. One was Ian and Jared bounding into the kitchen, ready to start the new day with breakfast. And outside they heard the sound of a helicopter. A few moments later they heard another. And then another.

"What's that?" Ian asked, startled by the noise.

"Helicopters," Lloyd and Trudy said in unison and then laughed at the timing of their simultaneous answers. The interlude of laughter was like a welcome cup of hot coffee on a cold morning. "At least we can still laugh," Trudy said.

The boys wanted to dash outside to see the helicopters. Lloyd and Trudy exchanged worried parental glances over their heads. The magnitude of just how much their world had changed since bedtime last night was just starting to sink in. "Sit down, guys," Lloyd said gently. "We have to talk."

For the next few minutes Trudy and Lloyd did their best both to define and to deflect the impact the storm would have on all their lives. They explained that the storm had caused a lot of trouble for a lot of people. The helicopters were on their way to rescue people trapped in their homes by the flood waters and the fallen trees blocking streets. Calmly and carefully, they recited the facts as they knew them and encouraged the boys to ask questions.

Ever the teacher, Trudy had a flashback to the workshop she'd attended as part of her in-service training. The event was intended to help school administrators and classroom teachers respond to children who'd undergone some sort of family trauma. "Impression without expression can lead to depression," the workshop leader had repeated throughout the session. Trudy felt much better than she had a few minutes ago now that she was focusing on what her boys needed instead of the damage outside.

The boys listened with wide-eyed fascination to the description of the downed trees, the blocked roads, the water coming into homes, and the adventure of living like pioneers with no power in the house. "Just like when we go camping in the mountains?" asked Ian. "Yes, but we get to sleep in beds, and we won't ride for hours in a car to get there," Trudy said.

"They can swim in their own basements?" Jared wondered.

"No they can't, sweetheart. The water isn't safe to be in. We can't even drink it right now. Make sure you do not drink any water without asking us first. Not even to brush your teeth."

The boys were visibly trying to grasp what this calamity would mean for them. The good news from their perspective was a reprieve from school for at least a couple of days. The bad news was no television and no computer games. But their handheld videogames would work as long as the batteries were charged, so that would be OK. They weren't sure what they thought about their favorite tree being down. When they went outside in their rain slickers to see the many puddles and the broken limbs, they gawked at their favorite play tree. The boys agreed it would be easier to climb on now and might make a pretty cool clubhouse. They didn't understand that their tree would be cleared away as soon as possible.

Meanwhile, other families from Emanuel were taking stock of their own situations. Preschool director Monica and her husband, Wayne, woke to the sound of howling winds. They'd slept peacefully through the storm until a neighbor's wind chime crashed through their dining-room window at 5:00 A.M. By then, the water from the flooding Green River was beginning to lap at their front door. News articles would later report that in this storm, places flooded that had never before flooded in recorded history. Their new home ended up with three feet of water on the first floor.

Once Monica and Wayne realized what was happening, they raced to round up towels and anything else they could find to hold the water back. But the water's determination to penetrate their home was greater than their ability to keep it at bay. With a sinking feeling, they resigned themselves to the destruction to come and retreated to the second floor. So as not to awaken the children, Danny and Benjamin, they took blankets and pillows into the boys' bedroom and waited for dawn.

Evelyn, Emanuel's office manager, woke up as usual at 6:30 A.M. and prepared for another long day at the church, now a Red Cross shelter. Since she never bothered to turn on lights or anything else until she was fully dressed and ready for breakfast, her first inkling that something was wrong came when the coffeemaker wouldn't start. She flipped the kitchen light switch. No light. She checked the phone. No dial tone. She tried her cell phone. No signal. She looked outside. Her neighborhood had been spared the worst of the wind damage, so at first glance everything looked normal.

She shrugged and decided to get her first cup of start-up juice from her favorite drive-through on the way to Emanuel. The power occasionally went out in her subdivision when others still had power. It was a minor inconvenience she'd learned to live with over the years. Now she was glad she'd been so exhausted the previous evening that she'd left her car in the driveway. With no power, the electric garage-door opener was useless, and there was no way to access the manual override inside the garage. It occurred to her that she needed to get someone out to add a window, or even a side door, so she wouldn't be locked out of her garage the next time the power failed. Before she started the car, she prayed she'd have the strength to do whatever needed to be done that day. She smiled as she thought to ask God for both kinds of power—the kind God provides directly and the kind the power-and-light company sells.

She suspected she'd probably be dealing with bad news all day, so rather than turn on a radio news program, she pushed the "play" button on her car's stereo CD system. She headed off to work to the sound of John Denver singing about country roads and Rocky Mountain highs. Those few moments of calm would be the last ones she'd know for many stressful hours to come.

As soon as Evelyn turned onto the main street that led to Emanuel, she saw how far conditions were from normal. She saw helicopters overhead, and police and volunteer firefighters at the intersections waving cars and people through. She turned on the morning news. The first report she heard made her stop in the middle of the road with her mouth open. A minute later Officer Dennis Prandle, the policeman directing traffic, came over to tell her to get moving. She introduced herself as one of the staff members from Emanuel who had been at the "Are You Ready?" event a couple of months ago. He'd been one of the presenters. She told him she was on her way to the church and asked if she could get there. Emanuel had opened as a Red Cross shelter, she explained, and she wanted to check on how folks were doing. He apologized for not remembering her and suggested the safest route, cautioning that the power was probably going to be out. "Good luck!" he said, waving her through.

Evelyn had a sinking feeling when she pulled into her parking spot and didn't see any lights on in the building. Lloyd, Monica, Evelyn, and other Emanuel leaders had carefully and prayerfully worked through a disaster preparation and response plan. The plan served them well in the hours leading up to the disaster. However, all the plans depended on their being able to communicate with one another throughout the disaster. Without power, they were without the Internet and maybe without phone service. Even their cell phones were not working—a wrinkle they hadn't anticipated. Now, rather than being "in the loop" and on top of the situation, they were cut off from one another, each wondering what to do and how to reach other key leaders. Though Emanuel's DPR team members had thought carefully about what they might encounter in a disaster, all their plans were based on the assumption that they'd be able to talk to each other. Now they realized that communications outages were also a significant part of disasters—and a source of anxiety on top of the rising water, the record levels of rain, and the high winds. They were already stressed and exhausted from all the excitement of getting ready for the pending disaster.

A Decision to Make

Should Evelyn stay at the office once she realizes there is no power at the church? The Emanuel DPR team had discussed what role Evelyn should play if Emanuel was affected by a disaster. The plan specified that she should call Pastor Albright or one of the other team members. They hadn't factored in the possibility that neither cell phones nor landline phones would work, so she had to decide for herself what to do. She knew the Emanuel Red Cross volunteers would be at church, but she also worried that they would be swamped with the many details necessary to take care of shelter residents.

The DPR plan had also assumed that Emanuel would hold worship services regardless of the situation, since congregation members would need and want to be together. The double-whammy of damage from both rising water and wind-driven rain was resulting in more headaches than any of the team had anticipated. Now Evelyn had to decide whether to stay at the church.

Yes, Evelyn should stay at the church.

- She knew the congregation's members better than anyone else available. The Red Cross shelter volunteer staff would be counting on her experienced and calm presence to help them manage the shelter.
- More people were likely to make their way to the shelter, and she could volunteer to fill in wherever the Red Cross volunteers most needed her.
- Emanuel members who could get there might show up as well, and she could help them, or direct them to Red Cross volunteers who might need their help with the shelter operation.

No, there is little she can do at the office.

- The Red Cross volunteer staff people would have the shelter under control and probably wouldn't really need her. Maybe her time would better spent doing something else.
- She wanted to check in on Lloyd and maybe the other Emanuel staff members. She figured she could ask a police officer to help her find the best routes to all their homes.
- She realized there was little she could do sitting in an office with no lights, no fans, no copier, no computer, no instructions on whether to plan for weekend services or cancel them, and no e-mail or phone communications.

Maybe. She could stay awhile to evaluate the situation and then decide.

- Evelyn believed someone ought to be there to meet and greet other people who might come in but who weren't checking into the shelter.

- She could wait to see if enough congregational members showed up to staff the shelter. That would free her up to make the rounds of other staff people.
- She could drive the short distance to Cindy's home and, if things were OK there, ask Cindy to come to the office while Evelyn checked on how her staff friends and colleagues were doing.
- She could see if one of the Red Cross volunteers would welcome any parishioners who might make their way to the church for whatever reasons.

What You Need to Know about . . .

DISASTER COMMUNICATIONS

Communication is often a major challenge in a disaster, whether natural or manmade, because power may be out for some time. Disasters also may compromise cell-phone towers and networks, making cell-phone signals unreliable. Landline phones that depend on electricity won't work either. In addition, as large numbers of people try to call into or out of the disaster area, the lines become overloaded. Emergency-response personnel will have specialized equipment to work around this contingency, but the average citizen will most likely be cut off from others.

1. Old-fashioned phones that plug directly into a telephone jack, and do not require an AC adapter, can run off power supplied through the telephone lines. These phones may work, assuming the phone lines themselves have not been damaged. Consider gathering a supply of older, simpler phones as part of your congregational disaster plan.
2. Text messages may go through when voice messages will not. However, it is wise to keep a cell phone turned off as much as possible, turning it on only to send or check for messages, as there will be no way to recharge the bat-

tery after it is drained—unless you have a battery-operated cell-phone charger.

3. Some people in disaster areas have had success with "smartphones" (handheld voice and e-mail electronic devices—the BlackBerry is one well-known brand name) that work when other forms of cell phones do not.
4. Battery-operated cell-phone chargers and portable radios powered by hand-cranking will work without electricity. Consider having these on hand as part of your disaster communications plan.
5. Gasoline-powered generators can provide enough power to run computers and other electronic equipment. However, generators are dangerous if not closely and skillfully monitored. Getting gasoline also becomes an issue when power goes out. Gas stations may run out of fuel, and can't pump what they have if they lose power.
6. As an alternative to relying on usual forms of communication, consider having walkie-talkies available to distribute to key disaster volunteer leaders.
7. Consider identifying people in your congregation and neighborhoods who are ham radio operators. These members are often able to provide vital communication links when other means of communication fail.
8. Designate a time and place to gather as soon as possible in a disaster, with the understanding that those who can get there will do so. Those who do not show up are put on a list of people to check in with as soon as possible.
9. Collect phone numbers and e-mail addresses for out-of-area friends or relatives for each person in the congregation considered an essential leader. Their families may be the first to know the whereabouts of these people and be eager to be a part of the communications chain.
10. Get to know your local government officials and first responders before a disaster strikes. Ask them how to relay critical information to your members should you lose usual forms of

communication. These officials will probably be grateful for the chance to teach you, and appreciate your offer to assist them in their work.

Implications for Your Congregation

Congregations have the opportunity to be an important part of local disaster response both by networking with other community disaster personnel and by helping to prepare their own people for disasters. Here are some issues to consider:

- Congregational leaders should be urged to talk with family members about family priorities before a disaster happens. Disaster-recovery efforts depend on volunteers to help shoulder the enormous burden of helping a community. However, congregation members also have commitments to their families, and may have already made commitments to employers, employees, and others.
- Disaster response and recovery is a long process. Encourage those who get involved in disaster-response ministry to pace themselves so that they do not create a domestic disaster by focusing on helping others while neglecting their own families. It is easy to do: every person one meets in a disaster has a heart-wrenching story and a long list of unmet needs.
- Disasters disrupt every aspect of life. Expect people to vacillate from extreme heroism and an attitude that "this won't defeat me" to helplessness and a mind-set that "this is overwhelming, and I can't cope." Expect both attitudes to surface many times—sometimes within a single hour.
- When you are engaged in disaster-response work, expect communications to be confusing and contradictory. Multiple layers of paid professionals and trained volunteers will quickly enter the area to begin offering humanitarian relief. Though they try diligently to coordinate efforts, they are working

against unknown and unpredictable obstacles. Relief workers cannot possibly know in advance the scope of the damage they will encounter, such as which routes for relief supply trucks will be accessible. In such circumstances, relief-work leaders will repeatedly adjust their outgoing messages about the on-the-ground situation. This array of conflicting information may lead people to think, "They don't what they're doing," an impression that contributes to an already high level of chaos and panic. To add to this confusion, although officials may be doing an excellent job of giving updates, citizens whose power is out may have no access to this information.

- Don't overlook the ancient communication system known as "word of mouth" when other modes of communication are impossible. Post signs on doors and bulletin boards, and walk the streets to pass along information and flyers. If you can't find a generator to power up a copier to make flyers, make them with markers or crayons. Taking flyers to public places that are operating can be effective both for distributing information and for calming anxieties. Make generous use of the disclaimer, "as far as we know at this time." Conditions change rapidly in a disaster zone. What may be true at a 10:00 A.M. briefing about distribution of food and water, for example, may not be true by 4:00 P.M.
- Do a fact check before passing along the rumors that will surely surface. That a story is repeated frequently does not mean that it is true. When people are anxious, they easily believe the worst stories that circulate. Leaders can do much to avert further panic by offering to get the facts and refusing to help rumors spread.
- Conference calls scheduled before the disaster occurs can be used to address a variety of disaster-related needs. When Hurricane Ike was approaching the Texas coast, the staff and rapid -response team of the Gulf Coast Synod of the Evangelical Lutheran Church in America set up a daily conference call, using

the same dial-in information and the same hour of the day for each call. After the storm, those who could call in, did.

- Consider establishing a partner congregation near your geographic area—but far enough away that its members are not likely to experience the same disaster, perhaps in an adjoining county. This partner faith community might become a place you could go to access Internet and phone communication should your own neighborhood suffer a prolonged power outage.

Resources

Kim Haddow and George Haddow, ***Disaster Communications in a Changing Media World*** (Burlington, Mass.: Butterworth-Heinemann, 2008). A handy reference on how to manage communications in a chaotic disaster situation.

Metropolitan Emergency Response and Logistical Information Network, *www.ndcrt.org*. A website devoted to helping nonprofit organizations with technical assistance, equipment, and manpower to respond to disasters.

Questions for Reflection

1. What's the longest stretch of time you've had to function without electricity and all the conveniences in your home that will not work without it? How did you manage that situation?
2. What equipment do you have on hand in case of a power loss? Flashlights? Camping lanterns? Hurricane lamps? Generators? Other?
3. What is your earliest memory of phone service? Describe the first telephone you remember using.
4. What sources do you use most often to get daily news reports? What alternatives are available to you when you can't access these?

5. Spend some time with family members or friends playing the "what if" exercise: think of all the potential disrupting events that could occur in your community. For each incident anyone suggests, brainstorm how you could manage if it happened.
6. How would you communicate with others if you had no working cell phone or landline phone?
7. What would want to do first if you experienced an emergency that cut you off from your place of work and the people you normally see every day?

Scripture Reflection

For everything there is a season, and a time for every matter
under heaven: a time to be born, and a time to die;
a time to plant, and a time to pluck up what is planted; . . .
a time to break down, and a time to build up;
a time to weep, and a time to laugh; . . .
a time to cast away stones, and a time to gather stones together.
—Ecclesiastes 3:1–5 RSV

CHAPTER 4

Calm Down!

EMOTIONAL RESPONSES IN A DISASTER

I waited patiently for the L*ORD;*
he turned to me and heard my cry.
He lifted me out of the slimy pit,
out of the mud and mire;
he set my feet on a rock
and gave me a firm place to stand.
—Psalm 40:1–3

Timeline

Later Thursday morning through Thursday evening. Evelyn stayed at the church and worked by a combination of flashlight and candlelight.

Situation

Evelyn greeted a steady stream of people coming to the church office. Hundreds of Green County residents spent the morning evacuating, or started the formidable task of removing the mountains of storm debris from their neighborhoods. However, some who had little damage to their homes overcame their sense of isolation by getting in their cars and driving around. Even some who had plenty of work to do at home felt compelled to see if there was anything they could do out in the community, or to take in the situation for themselves.

Emanuel was located in an area that had sustained less damage than many others. Driving past, some Emanuel members saw cars in the church parking lot and pulled in to find out what was going on. Some of them felt a strong urge to be around familiar people. Pastor Lloyd Albright arrived around 11:00 A.M. Despite the large tree that had fallen across the driveway, he had been able to maneuver the car out. Trudy had rebounded from feeling overwhelmed and stunned. The boys' enthusiasm had given her a fresh shot of energy and resolve to be brave and stay calm for their sake. She knew Lloyd wouldn't be able to focus on matters at home until he knew how things were at Emanuel. She encouraged him to go see for himself.

After he and Evelyn had exchanged stories about the day so far, Evelyn suggested he go back home to make some phone calls, since the landline at his house was working. Lloyd had all the phone numbers he'd need on his cell phone. While he couldn't make phone calls with it, the directory portion of it was working fine. She would stay at the office for the next few hours.

As Lloyd was leaving, John Sullivan, a member of Emanuel's DPR team and a retired phone company manager, stopped by to offer his assistance. He said he thought he could round up a few phones for the church office that wouldn't require electricity. He took on the task of finding them and promised he'd make his first call to Lloyd if he succeeded.

Before John was even out of the building, Helen Wilson stopped by the office. A retired nurse, she had worked at a drug-and-alcohol rehab center between Caldwell and Yorkshire. Working with people whose lives were in chaos from various addictions had taught her to stay calm amid chaos. She seemed undaunted by the destruction all around her. The retirement community where she lived had lost power, but little else was damaged. Given her good fortune, her automatic response was to focus on helping others less fortunate.

Seeing Evelyn and Lloyd, she sensed they were already feeling the strain of trying to do too much under trying circumstances.

Although Helen had no electricity in her apartment, she had everything she needed to put together a decent meal, so she invited Evelyn and Lloyd home for lunch.

"You two need a break!" she announced. "You won't make it to Sunday if you keep going at this pace. Let me feed you. It'll do you both good to get out of this building for a little bit. Besides, if the power doesn't come on for a few days, I'll have to get rid of everything in the fridge and freezer anyway."

"But Trudy is waiting for me," Lloyd objected. "And I can't call her to tell her I'll be late."

"It's not the first time and it surely won't be the last time that's happened," Evelyn said. "Can we pack up a 'to go' lunch for her and the boys?" she asked Helen.

"Of course."

"Then I agree. I could sure use a calm place for a few minutes." Turning to Lloyd, she added, "I really need to talk some things over with you, and we can't do it here. It's been a nonstop parade of people this morning. I clocked it—fifteen minutes without drop-ins is the record so far."

"That long?" asked Helen. "You know, those interruptions are the ministry right now. People just want to see for themselves that their house of worship and the people they trust are going to be available to them."

"I hadn't quite thought of it that way," Evelyn admitted. "I was so focused on how I'd do all the things that need to get done."

"I think everything is up for grabs at the moment," Lloyd said. "We're all OK. Our homes are functional. Our families are safe. OK. I do need a sanity break. Thank you, Helen. St. Helen to the rescue! What's for lunch?"

Over fruit, sandwiches, chips, and bottled lemonade, Helen praised Evelyn and Lloyd for their outreach to those in need. Then she warned them not to do too much at the expense of their own well-being.

"This disaster is bigger than all of us together," she said. "We'll never get through it if we spend all our energy in the first week. I care about both of you too much to watch you burn out. Besides, I need my congregation to survive this. So you know there's no such thing as a free lunch. The cost of this lunch is a commitment that you'll take care of yourselves."

Lloyd and Evelyn groaned. "We've been had, Evelyn," Lloyd said in mock despair. "No one ever won an argument with this woman!"

"Good. Now, what day next week are you taking off?" Helen asked, looking at both of them.

They both rolled their eyes and agreed that, though they didn't know yet when they could take a day off, they'd make a commitment to do it.

Helen packed a lunch for Trudy and the boys. She asked Lloyd to offer a prayer for them all, especially the rescue workers arriving in town, and sent them off with a hug and a thank-you for coming over.

Lloyd went home to make phone calls. Fortunately, he had a pretty good list of alternate phone numbers for most of his key leaders. Evelyn headed back to the church, hoping the activity associated with the Red Cross shelter wouldn't result in too many interruptions.

Peg Mitchell was sitting in her car waiting for Evelyn. Emanuel's self-appointed overseer of everyone else's well-being, Peg could be a bit overbearing and excessive in her enthusiasm for sharing her faith with others—whether they were interested or not. But she was usually the first to inform the office when someone went into the hospital, lost a job, lost a relative, or met with any other affliction. She meant well, Evelyn would say in Peg's defense. Most of the time Evelyn and the rest of the staff appreciated her efforts and tried to tone down her fervor for promoting Emanuel in the community.

On his calmer days Pastor Albright thought of Peg as his "Triple E" member—Extra Enthusiastic Evangelist. At other times he wished he could help her understand that her zeal to share her love of God sometimes came across as intrusive and unwelcome rather than inviting. He figured there was little chance of that, so he accepted the updates on members and refrained from challenging her style of recruiting souls for the kingdom.

Let Your Actions Do the Talking

It cannot be stressed often enough that a disaster site is not the place to evangelize or proselytize. It's ineffective to talk theology with someone distracted by the losses and fears they've just experienced. People of varying religious backgrounds have different ideas about God's connection to a disaster. It is inappropriate to argue about these differences with a disaster survivor. Disaster chaplains consider it unethical to pressure someone made vulnerable by disaster into a religious conversation.

The best way to share your faith in a disaster zone is to show up with a caring heart, a listening ear, and an offer for tangible help—say, a drink of water or a cup of coffee.

Take your cues from disaster survivors. If they want to talk, be prepared to listen. If they don't or can't talk right away, just be present with them. Asking open-ended questions and listening is more effective than trying to teach or persuade.

See appendix C for more specific ways to offer spiritual and emotional care to disaster survivors.

Evelyn was appalled but hardly surprised that Peg jumped right in: "This is a great chance for our congregation to be seen in the community. We've got to set up a relief tent. We can pass out water and food baskets. People will be so grateful! I figure I will need a thousand dollars to go get ice and food. Oh, and we'll need some brochures, so people will know about Emanuel. If we jump on this, we can have it in place maybe even today."

Evelyn tried to explain why this effort might not be possible, but Peg wasn't persuaded. Finally, in frustration, Evelyn directed Peg to Faith Monroe in the wing of the building being used for the Red

Cross shelter. She felt a bit guilty about doing so, but Faith had said repeatedly, "I'm here. Use me. I've been through this before."

Be Prepared

Disaster-response professionals stress the need for each household to keep an emergency kit handy. Such a kit should contain sufficient provisions of food, water, medications, and other basics for the first seventy-two hours of a disaster. It can take that long for emergency supplies to reach an affected region. The disaster could render roads impassable, or a toxic spill or out-of-control fire could hinder the mobility of the disaster-response staff.

Disasters often leave a community without electrical power for some time. The power outage could continue for days or even weeks. Plan meals that require only a manual can opener or scissors to open and prepare. Then make sure you have those tools in your emergency kit—unless you enjoy eating thawed, uncooked microwave meals. (People fortunate enough to have stoves with gas burners and ovens may have the luxury of hot meals.)

For complete lists of items to pack in an emergency kit, see appendix B.

As Evelyn was making a list of things she might be able to do by flashlight and candlelight, another member came by to see her. This time it was Irene Hunter, newly retired and the self-appointed chief of the Thursday newsletter crew— the half-dozen retirees who usually showed up to help every Thursday at 2:00 P.M. Irene was a few hours early today. The volunteer crew was a tremendous help to the office staff, but the women also counted on this time for their weekly social gathering.

Most of the Thursday folders were residents of the same retirement community where Helen Wilson lived. This apartment building, where some other Emanuel members also lived, was without power, as was much of the rest of the county, but it did have emergency generators to provide for the basics. The staff could provide adequate medical care and food service. Residents could gather in the community room for support and socializing. The generators were not used to power individual TVs, radios, or any other nonessentials in private apartments. The real challenge was that the plumbing was operating at minimal capacity. Lack of power also meant lack of infrastructure—including sewage systems. For the time being, showers, baths, and flushing were off limits.

For these retirement community residents, life was good in that they were safe, had each other, and were surrounded by staff available to tend to any emergency needs. However, daily routines were disrupted, and many residents were more restless than usual. Unable to phone the church and not knowing whether there would be worship on Sunday, Irene had decided to drive over to see what was going on there.

Evelyn told Irene that no decision had been made yet about worship services, and even if there were a Sunday service, it would be impossible to print the bulletins without electricity. However, in Evelyn's usual organized way, the monthly newsletters had already been printed and were ready to fold. She asked Irene if she thought the Thursday folders would want to work on these back at the retirement center. That sounded good to Irene. She and Evelyn put the newsletters in Irene's car.

Few members of the congregation knew all that Evelyn did behind the scenes to keep the ministries of the church working smoothly. What they did know was that she was usually calm, efficient, and available to them—at least during reasonable working hours.

When Irene returned to the retirement center, the crew was grateful for this excuse to gather. The women set up shop in the community room and were soon busy folding newsletters and swapping stories. The soft glow of many battery-operated lanterns added a pleasant ambience to their weekly fold-and-chat session. For this group of women, the telephone was the main way to stay in touch with friends and family. While the retirement center had phone service, many of the people they wanted to call did not, and after the storm and howling winds last night, they were ready to talk.

And talk they did. Given that the retirement community was well outside the flood area, they were among the safest citizens in Caldwell. Nonetheless, they found the news about the extensive flooding and wind damage in the community unsettling. They worried about people they couldn't reach by phone. They worried about the people in local shops and businesses where they went on weekly outings. They worried about a great many things.

When they finished their folding, Irene went back to her apartment. All the people they had just talked about kept running through her mind. She couldn't remember when she'd felt so restless. More out of habit than any conscious decision, she picked up the phone and dialed Emanuel's number. She got a message referring her to Pastor Albright's home number in case of emergency. "Is this an emergency?" she asked herself. "Of course it is. Some of these people can't take care of themselves. I have to do something!" She dialed the Albrights' number.

To his surprise and relief, Lloyd was able to reach a few people on his landline. Some members reported moderate damage to their property—trees down, power out, fences down. One member had a tree fall on her car. Another reported that her home was mostly all right, but when she tried to report for work, a security officer turned her away, saying the basement of the building had flooded, and the office would be closed for at least several days.

Reaching some of the DPR team members, Lloyd explained that many of the people he had tried to call didn't have phone service. A couple of people offered to drive around to check on members. Lloyd suggested they wait until tomorrow to see what would happen next. "One thing, though—we have to rethink how our VC phone network gets used."

While he was looking up another number, the phone rang. Irene's voice sounded anxious at the other end. "Pastor, some of us at the retirement center have been talking. We've got some people we're worried about. What should we do?"

Lloyd sighed. He knew it would be pointless to suggest they not worry. Worrying was part of how they took care of each other. He asked, "Well, who are these people?" Irene went down the list. Lloyd knew most of the people, but a few names were unfamiliar to him. "Do you know if any of them registered with the county special-needs program?" She didn't know.

"Well, Irene, I don't think we have enough people to just drive around right now—and too many of the roads either aren't open or have checkpoints. Only emergency personnel are allowed past them. I know it's hard, but I really think the best thing any of us can do right now is to say our prayers and sit this out for a while. Besides, I've been on the phone with some of our DPR team members. We're contacting everyone we can who has phone service. I know this is tough. But we've been through tough times before. I know you certainly have."

Irene sighed. This wasn't the answer she wanted to hear. "I guess you're right. Will we have church Sunday?"

"I don't know yet. I'll have to talk it over with a few people. It's hard to get much of anything done when so many people are without phone service. I'm surprised you got through. I can't even access the church directory on my computer, or print out my sermon notes."

"That's one advantage of not upgrading to every new gadget that comes along. My manual typewriter works just fine, thank you very much."

"Well, if I need to finish my sermon, I may be asking to borrow it."

"Of course. You know I'd be happy to lend it to you. Do you want to come pick it up now?" She was hoping to see him in person but reluctant to say so.

"I'd love to see you, Irene. But for the moment I think I'd better stay here, and you'd better stay there." He asked her if she'd like a prayer before he hung up. She did indeed. He offered a short prayer, thanking God for bringing Irene and her friends through the storm safely and asking God's peace and courage for those who were suffering now.

Curiosity Hampers the Rescue Effort

As soon as it appears that the danger from a disaster has subsided, most of us are curious to see what happened. People with official responsibilities who can move about without putting themselves or others in harm's way can be a source of help to the first responders on the scene.

However, sightseers eager to see the damage for themselves can impede the progress of the rescue and relief organizations that are moving people and equipment into place. Local government officials will put out a plea for volunteer help as soon as such help is needed and they are ready to receive it.

Lloyd continued to wonder whether Emanuel should try to hold worship services on Sunday. He tried to call a couple of other pastors in the area to find out how they were doing and to see if they intended to hold services. Unable to reach any of them, he called back the handful of Emanuel council and DPR folks he'd reached before. Six of them agreed to gather at the Albright home that evening. They wanted to review their situation and talk about whether to hold services on Sunday.

Evelyn looked up from her desk to find Peg waiting for her. She'd gone in search of a store that would sell or donate supplies. Of course, most places were closed. The few that weren't had long lines and limited inventories. Along the way Peg had been listening to the radio. The news was bad—tragic stories of people flooded out of their homes, stuck in long lines of slow-moving traffic for hours, stranded on their roofs or in their attics; critical-care facilities without electricity and operating on generators that were rapidly using up limited supplies of gasoline. More than a dozen homes had caught fire and burned beyond repair because fire departments couldn't maneuver through all the fallen trees. A couple of homes had been struck by lightning; the other fires were the result of people's leaving burning candles unattended. There were also tragic reports of inexperienced users of generators dying of carbon-monoxide poisoning.

Hearing the news reports bolstered Peg's resolve to use the Emanuel parking lot as a distribution center. Although Faith Monroe had explained that FEMA (the Federal Emergency Management Agency) would be setting up points of distribution (PODs) by tomorrow, Peg was sure that FEMA's efforts wouldn't be enough.

Coffee, Anyone?

FEMA frequently uses the parking lots of churches or other faith-based organizations to set up its POD operations. This setup may bring hundreds of people into contact with a faith community. The arrangement offers a unique opportunity to reach out to neighbors. Pastor Liz Stein is one Houston pastor whose church's parking lot became a neighborhood POD site following Hurricane Ike. Zion Lutheran was without power, so making coffee there wasn't an option. However, when power was restored at her house, she quickly found her niche. The church owned several large portable coffee urns. It became her morning routine to fill these at home. On her way to the church she would stop off at a bakery for kolaches and sweet rolls. Then she distributed the hot coffee and pastries to the eagerly waiting FEMA workers. She quickly became known in the neighborhood as "the pastor with the coffee and kolaches."

Evelyn found herself getting angrier and more frustrated by the minute, inundated by a seemingly endless list of needs she couldn't meet and a long list of routine tasks she couldn't accomplish under these less-than-idyllic circumstances. She was about to find some excuse to leave when John Sullivan came down the hallway humming a tune. "Look what I found!" he said, beaming as he placed two plain black telephones on her desk.

"Will they work?" Evelyn asked.

"Don't know, but I'm about to find out." He disappeared under a table and started working his way through a maze of wires to find the wall jack for the phone. A minute later, they agreed that the dial tone was the sweetest sound they'd heard all day. As he'd promised, his first call was to Pastor Albright. Lloyd let out a yelp of excitement and said he'd head over to the office right away.

The next person to show up was Fred Gleason, chair of Emanuel's property committee. He reported a damp spot in the ceiling and one on a section of wall in the worship space, plus a soggy section of carpet. The wind the previous night had blown out a window that needed to be boarded up. And the roof had a leak.

Evelyn groaned. She'd been so busy that she hadn't even left the office complex to see the worship space. Fred insisted that the building would need immediate attention and asked Evelyn to give him a purchase order so he could go get the materials. A blue tarp would do for now—but the damage had to be repaired as soon as possible. "Mold, you know," he said. Evelyn reminded Fred she didn't have the authority to approve the purchase. She made a mental note to add "purchasing" to the list of things the DPR team had to address. Who *does* have the authority to make decisions and spend money in a disaster? That item had been overlooked. Fred fumed out of the office, muttering under his breath about people who were too cheap to put up a decent roof, back when they had the chance. "I told them this would happen if they tried to cut corners on the reroofing project," he said to no one in particular.

Next in line was Lacy Rogers. "I've been calling you all day. Why wasn't anyone here to answer the phones?"

"Our phones were out. John Sullivan just got me set up with this old landline. Do you have phone service?"

"Yes, of course. I didn't know you didn't."

"Haven't you been listening to the news? We're in the middle of a disaster. We don't have power. We didn't have phones until a few minutes ago." Evelyn was working overtime to be patient with Lacy, whose ability to remain serenely unaware of any situation that didn't directly affect her was truly impressive. Today it was also annoying.

"The news always exaggerates things. Of course, I know there was a storm. But my neighborhood is pretty much OK. I figured the few people who insist on living by the river take their chances. This time, they got flooded. They should all have insurance. Actually, it's the storm that brought me in here. I'm just wondering if the finance committee meeting is still on for tonight. I mean, I know there have been a lot of trees downed and everything, but there wasn't any flooding in my neighborhood, and that's where most of the committee members live. We can't afford to just skip a month. We're going to have a lot of extra expenses. Who knows what we'll have to spend to clean up the mess around here? We can't afford to postpone this meeting. Has anyone made a decision? Where is Pastor Albright when we need him? Why isn't he here? If this is a disaster, you'd think he'd be here."

Evelyn explained that Lloyd had been working at home, where he had phone service, and that he was now on his way into the office. Lacy sighed and sat down to wait for more information.

Evelyn nearly cried from relief when she heard Lloyd's voice talking to one of the Red Cross volunteers down the hall. As soon as he appeared in the office, she escorted him by candlelight to his office and started down the list of things that had happened since their respite lunch with Helen only hours ago.

His first official duty after that was to tell Lacy, as calmly and forcefully as he could, that the meeting for tonight was off. "Will you put up a sign saying so in case anyone thinks it's on?" he asked. Lacy protested briefly, agreed to do so, and reminded him that she'd need receipts for all the extra expenses.

The conversation about expenses reminded Lloyd that he had totally—and uncharacteristically—forgotten in all the turmoil that he had been planning to go out of town this weekend for his annual continuing-education event. The council members had assured him that they could handle worship for him, but in the wake of the storm he didn't feel right about going. Because of the event's location this year, he and Trudy had hoped to use the trip as a mini-vacation for the family. He added that to his growing list of decisions to make.

By now both Evelyn and Lloyd were too weary and distracted to accomplish much, so they took their candles and flashlights and made their way through the darkened hallways to the kitchen. Volunteers were busy preparing dinner for the shelter residents. Mercifully, the kitchen had gas stoves, which were still working. A combination of forty-eight men, women, and children were resigned to calling the Emanuel fellowship and education wing home for a while. They couldn't go home, and for the most part they were too stunned to think clearly enough to make other arrangements. The Red Cross volunteers knew they'd have to start nudging people to make plans soon, but for now, they were concentrating on trying to help the visitors feel at home in the makeshift shelter.

The Red Cross volunteers greeted Lloyd and Evelyn with hugs and an offer of leftover coffee. One of the volunteers had made coffee on the gas stove, since the electric coffeemakers would be out of commission until the power came back on.

Evelyn grasped her cup and clung to it like a life preserver. She so admired the generosity of these volunteers. They were all doing the best they could. She suspected that some of them had their own storm-related problems to deal with at home. "You are the salt of the earth," she told one of them as she took a sip of the coffee and involuntarily made a face. It was warm, but that was about all it had going for it.

The volunteer grinned at her. "We go for quantity, not quality, 'round these parts, ma'am." It had been a long time since any of the volunteers on duty had made coffee in anything other than modern coffeemakers. They were accustomed to the kind where all one had to do was place a pre-measured pack of coffee in the basket and push the "start" button.

"Looks like we're in for some learning curves," said Lloyd.

"Speaking of learning curves," said the volunteer, "you know the High Hill Supermarket where the Red Cross has credit to buy shelter food? Their windows all blew out, and they have no power. They're closed. We don't have an account at the only store in the area that's still open. Any bright ideas?"

"Yes. Call the Red Cross and tell them about it," said Evelyn. Lloyd nodded his approval.

"Sure, if we had a phone that worked," the volunteer said.

"Thanks be to God and John Sullivan, we do. Follow me," said Evelyn.

Lloyd followed Evelyn and the volunteer back to the office. While the volunteer called the Red Cross, Lloyd and Evelyn retreated to Lloyd's office to talk about their day. A half-hour later they completed a coping plan for the next twenty-four hours. Evelyn was to take tomorrow off. No excuses. No arguments. "Or I'll sic Helen on you," Lloyd threatened good-naturedly.

Since Trudy's school was closed and was not going to be used as a shelter, she and Lloyd would set up camp at the church tomorrow. Now that they had found a way to make and receive phone messages, he could be as useful there as anywhere. The boys could hang out in the nursery with the battery-operated lantern they had and enjoy a change of scenery. Maybe some of the kids staying at the shelter could join them. Trudy could be a real asset helping with the children. Lloyd said he'd make a decision about holding services Sunday after he talked with whichever DPR people showed up that night. He suggested that Evelyn take the extra phone John Sullivan had brought to the office, so they could talk tomorrow.

"It's quitting time," Lloyd announced as he checked his watch and saw that it was already 5:30. "Think you've had enough fun for one day?"

"Enough fun for at least a week's worth of days," she answered.

"Why don't you follow me home and let us feed you. I hate to see you eating alone after the day you've put in. Then we'll chase you home to do the Abe Lincoln thing and read by candlelight for the rest of the evening."

Evelyn agreed, and they made their way through the building together, thanking the volunteers and encouraging the shelter residents along the way.

A Decision to Make

Should Emanuel hold services on Sunday, given the damage to the sanctuary and Lloyd's scheduled continuing-education trip? The trip was paid for, and he was combining it with a weekend getaway with Trudy and the boys.

Disasters demand many decisions that have to be made quickly, often with spotty information and amid challenges. One critical role for religious leaders is to establish safe places for disaster survivors to gather, support one another, and tell their stories of what happened. Ideally, this gathering should happen within the first day. Emanuel was already offering such a gathering place on an informal basis.

Another decision facing Lloyd and the other leaders was whether to provide a more formal setting for people to gather. People of faith generally find familiar routines and rituals associated with worship reassuring. Yet Lloyd wondered if it was wise to try to hold worship in facilities damaged by wind and water, and without electricity. He was also wondering how to notify people about the decision of whether to have worship on Sunday.

Yes, of course they would have worship.

- People want and need to be together. They are eager to check in with one another and gain support and encouragement from a worship experience. The damage to the sanctuary is minor.
- This is a good time for the lay leadership of the church to help people remember that God's care is not determined by the condition of a building or expressed only through professional religious leaders. Anyone with compassion can provide spiritual first aid. They can worship with or without Pastor Albright's presence.
- Holding a worship service will show the members the work ahead of them to make repairs to the building.

No, the potential problems were too great.

- Until the building has been checked for mold, it is unwise to expose the more vulnerable members of the community to the sanctuary.
- Everyone in the congregation knows someone who needs help. Members should show their compassion by canceling worship and urging people to go help their neighbors.

Maybe there would be a way to have the service.

- Masks could be provided for those concerned about mold.
- The worship service could be modified to focus on a few psalms or other readings, use some inspiring hymns that most worshipers know well enough to sing by memory, include other meaningful elements of worship (such as the Lord's Prayer), and end by sending people out to serve their neighbors.

What You Need to Know about . . .

EMOTIONAL FALLOUT IN THE WAKE OF A DISASTER

The situation following a disaster will be chaotic and stressful. People who function best with a predictable structure may become agitated. People's typical personalities may be magnified. So, for example, usually shy people may totally clam up. Typically nervous people may become irritable and argumentative.

1. Information will be sparse and constantly changing. The dearth of hard facts will lead people to conclude that no one is in charge or in control and add to a sense of panic.
2. The auto-response to a life-threatening situation or one perceived to be life-threatening is to move into survival mode. High-order levels of thinking are bypassed. The ability to think

clearly and make logical decisions may be compromised. For example, an announcement about a potential shortage of ice can lead some people to decide that they must have ice right now, cannot live without it, and need to do whatever it takes to get theirs—even if they don't actually need any ice. When many people think this way, their collective mood can degenerate into a mob mentality.

3. Symptoms of stress and exhaustion are not always immediately evident. People may insist that they are doing "great" or "OK" when in reality they are not aware of the toll the stress is taking on them. For example, some people will be unable to make a decision, or appear helpless. Others may become aggressive, making unreasonable or irrelevant demands. Others may make rash or inappropriate choices.
4. As the stress continues, which it will for some time in a disaster, individuals may begin to exhibit physical symptoms. This is especially true for children, whose first symptom of stress may be a stomach-ache or headache. Children lack the vocabulary to talk about what they are experiencing. Children and adults alike may also suffer from insomnia or a generalized feeling of anxiety and worry. (Chapter 9 deals in more detail with issues of children and disaster trauma.)
5. Whole communities, as well as individuals, can experience stress reactions. The recognized leaders' ability to manage their own stress and anxiety directly affect whether people's symptoms of stress decrease or increase.
6. We are generally unaware of how much emotional influence we have on one another. If one person can remain calm while surrounded by anxious people, that individual can help reduce the overall sense of fear and panic in the crowd. Staying calm is not the same as being passive and disconnected. Rather, it means that the individual is able to speak slowly, deliberately, and calmly in response—but not in reaction—to the others in the situation.

7. Basic stress-management techniques are especially important in the midst of a disaster. Some of these are:

    - Breathe slowly.
    - Speak slowly and softly.
    - Count to ten before speaking.
    - Think about your response before you speak.
    - Be aware of your own emotional condition and how it might be influencing your thinking.
    - Take a break. Go for a walk. Take a nap. Read something that's not about the disaster.
    - Find something pleasant to focus on for a while. Move away from the news reports.

Implications for Your Congregation

Recovering from a disaster will most likely mean that your congregation will have to eliminate, postpone, or revise some of the programs you had in place before the event. This change of plans will require coordination when leaders are least likely to have time or energy to think creatively. That is why it's good to do as much disaster preparation as possible.

- People often turn to their faith communities following a disaster. If your regular worship space were not available, how could you conduct worship?
- If your pastor, rabbi, or other religious leader was unavailable to lead worship, how could your faith community gather and worship?
- Caregivers are susceptible to burnout following a community disaster. Before a disaster is the best time to think of ways to prevent burnout. One strategy to maximize the health and vitality of core leaders is to provide extra time off. This may be difficult to "sell" to these leaders, as they may

want to be, or people may expect them to be, closely engaged in the overall disaster-response efforts in addition their usual responsibilities.
- Disasters can have disastrous effects on a congregational budget. Congregational leaders will have to wrestle with how to fund extra, unanticipated expenses while expecting a reduction in giving as members cope with their own financial disasters. Disaster planning should include a contingency plan to meet unanticipated expenses.
- Making arrangements to implement conference calls for key leaders on an as-needed basis allows leaders to assess the situation quickly and decide how best to respond. Those members of the team who are unable to join the conference call are added to the list of people to track down as soon as possible.
- Consider establishing a partner relationship with a congregation near, but not in, your geographic area. You can agree to use each other's facilities for Internet and phone communication should either of you experience a power outage.

Resources

Stephen B. Roberts and Willard W. C. Ashley, ***Disaster Spiritual Care: Practical Clergy Responses to Community, Regional and National Tragedy*** (Woodstock, Vt.: Skylight Paths Publishing, 2008).

Kevin Massey, ***Light Our Way: A Guide for Spiritual Care in Times of Disaster for Disaster Response Volunteers, First Responders and Disaster Planners*** (Arlington, Va.: National Voluntary Organizations Active in Disaster, 2006).

Questions for Reflection

1. What kinds of situations do you find most stressful?
2. What helps you calm down when you feel stressed?

3. How do you typically respond when you're around someone who is obviously having a lot of stress in his or her life?
4. Have you had to deal with a stressful situation that lasted three or more months? If so, what impact did that have on you and those around you?
5. Who are among the calmest, most clear-thinking members of your congregation? Consider asking them to be available to answer phones in a time of disaster.
6. Following a disaster, some express their desire to be reassured by making demands for immediate attention and action. How could your congregation organize a rapid-response system to address this situation?

Scripture Reflection

Have no anxiety about anything, but in everything by prayer and supplication with thanksgiving let your requests be made known to God. And the peace of God, which passes all understanding, will keep your hearts and your minds in Christ Jesus.

—Philippians 4:6–7 RSV

CHAPTER 5

A Completely Different World

CONGREGATIONAL ROLES IN EARLY RELIEF EFFORTS

Do not forget to entertain strangers, for by so doing some people have entertained angels without knowing it.
—Hebrews 13:2

Timeline

Thursday evening and Friday morning. The decision is made to hold a different kind of worship service on Sunday.

Situation

Pastor Lloyd Albright went back to the dark office to call Trudy and let her know he was heading home and bringing Evelyn with him. Before he could get out the door, Faith tracked him down. "Pastor, FEMA needs places to set up their points of distribution. Do you think we could have one here? We already have the people who will need that help."

He acted on his first impulse: "Of course." He figured he'd deal with the details later. Right now all he wanted was to be at home with Trudy and the boys—even if the house was dark and dinner consisted of cold leftovers. "Besides," he told himself, "I know just the person to assign to help FEMA set this up." He chuckled as he pictured Peg trying to organize the entire FEMA staff.

Evelyn voiced her heartfelt thanks after dinner and headed home. Officer Prandle was still directing traffic in her neighborhood. She rolled down the car window and called out to him. "You gonna be doing this all night?"

He grinned. "I'm getting off easy. Only twelve-hour shifts for us these days. Pray for the utility guys. They're expected to be at work at five in the morning and go until eight or nine at night. Met one today from Butler, Pennsylvania. He's been away from home since the middle of August cleaning up where hurricanes have been knocking power out all over the place. Says they're putting the crew up at the Regency in Yorkshire. Sweet deal. Except they're never there long enough to enjoy it. Says only two more weeks to go till he gets to go home for a few days. This is rough—no denying that. I missed my coffee and doughnut break today."

"Wow. That is tough. Well, I'll sleep a couple of hours in your honor."

"Thanks. Be careful. Don't drink the water! Say, tell that preacher guy to pray for us. It's tough sending these young bucks into the messes we do. I got it easy just directing traffic. But some of them are gonna have nightmares after they see what's under all that muck."

"I promise." As Evelyn returned to her dark house, she resolved that somehow tomorrow she'd show her appreciation and support for Officer Prandle and his crew.

Earlier, while waiting for the Emanuel DPR team members to arrive, Trudy and Lloyd caught news updates on their battery-operated radio. The news was numbing. Over twenty-five hundred people had been flooded out of their homes. Roads all over the area were blocked by fallen trees. A dozen group-home residents died when the driver of the bus they were using to evacuate swerved to miss a fallen tree limb and lost control. The bus turned over.

The unofficial county death toll was over forty. Residents were unprepared for the destructive nature of high winds and floodwaters. Several died trying to drive through high water. When the water started to reach the level of their car windows, they tried to get out, but in most cases could not.

Power was out in communities from Houston to Chicago to Cleveland. The number of people without power was well into the millions, with no clear pattern to the outages. Some were without power for a few hours; others would have no electricity for days. The blackout included facilities that might normally be helpful to relief-and-recovery efforts—police stations, hospitals, schools, nursing homes, government offices. Critical facilities had generators, but these were sufficient only to run essential equipment. Everyone was feeling the effects of the storm in some way. News organizations were estimating that one in five families in the Green County area were either going to be homeless or be living in inadequate housing for some time to come.

Most Green County residents spent Thursday night either in a shelter, in the dark in their own homes, or, having evacuated, out of town. Everywhere they looked, people saw evidence that the Coast Guard and other first responders were moving into the region. They came from virtually every state in the union, plus a few from Canada. Relief workers in tractor trailers from FEMA, the American Red Cross, and the Salvation Army were a common sight.

After the sobering news reports the Albrights were hearing, they were relieved to hear the first knock on the door. By a quarter after seven, Lloyd and four members of the DPR team were assessing what had happened to each of them, their families, their church, and their community.

After the group spent thirty-five minutes exchanging stories by lantern and candlelight, Lloyd closed that part of the meeting with a prayer. He choked up several times trying to speak after so many accounts of great loss. He was deeply moved by the efforts of these faithful men and women. When he tried to thank them, Hal Beckman cut him off, saying, "If there was one thing I learned from Katrina, it's that we have to stick together. I saw my share of miracles after that disaster, and I expect we'll be seeing them here too. Just keep your eyes and ears open."

Cindy chimed in: "I think we're all just grateful we have our church family and you to lead us. I wouldn't feel right not doing what I could to help out now."

Jill Hanson and John Sullivan agreed. John added, "We need to pray for all those utility workers and people like Sammy who are out there in this mess working right now." It's definitely not fun, and sometimes it's downright dangerous what they do for us."

"Don't forget Faith and the folks over at the shelter," Jill added.

"Guess the Lord wouldn't mind hearing from us again so soon. Let us pray," Lloyd said and offered another prayer for all those who were already at work bringing aid and comfort to others.

Then they turned to discussing the best ways for Emanuel to respond to the disaster. The evening did much to renew Lloyd's wavering faith and to strengthen his resolve to be part of the relief-and-recovery effort from this setback. The group members quickly and unanimously agreed to have services on Sunday. People were hungry for community and some semblance of normality. The only debate was whether to "go ecumenical" by joining forces with neighboring congregations or to hold their own service.

They finally agreed they'd hold their own service this weekend and look into doing something with others the following Wednesday—the one-week anniversary of the flood and storm.

This decision was followed by a discussion on how best to put together a service, given that Emanuel had no electrical power, limited communication with members, and no way to announce plans. In addition, Lloyd was still undecided about his plans for the continuing education and family mini-vacation trip. He was supposed to be leaving Saturday. "I've already paid the full conference fee and booked the flights and hotel room. Trudy was really looking forward to this."

He admitted that he felt torn about calling off personal plans but didn't feel right about not staying with the Emanuel members at such a time. That decision was finally made when Jill pointed out that flights might not be back on schedule until early next week. The airport at Yorkshire had closed Wednesday and was still closed as of Thursday evening. The news anchor on one of the Yorkshire radio stations reported that airport officials weren't sure when flights would resume. The control tower had sustained a fair amount of damage from blown-out windows and water. Even if the airport were open, a huge backlog of passengers would be waiting to get a plane out.

After more discussion Lloyd said he'd try to get his money back from the conference planners. Surely they'd understand his need to be home now. John told him, "We expect you to take Trudy on a weekend away between now and the end of the year. If you happen also to learn something while you're away, that'd be great. But I suspect we're all going to be learning a lot of new things right here in Green County."

Lloyd thanked them for their support and offered yet another prayer—this one silently, thanking God for the generosity and encouragement of his members.

With that decision resolved, they worked out the plans for Sunday. They'd hold one service in the parking lot. That way, any passersby might feel comfortable joining them. This arrangement would also eliminate any mold issues. They'd post handwritten signs on the doors of the church. Jill offered to call Luke Avalon, chair of the children and youth task force, to suggest that he try to round up a few youth to make and post signs at any of the businesses or restaurants in town that were open. Jill suggested they do an e-mail blast if the power came back on. Cindy offered to help Hal use the VC phone tree to reach members who had phone service.

Next they moved to discussing how long to keep the Red Cross shelter open, how to find out who among their own members was in trouble, and what to do about the damage to the sanctuary.

After the group left, Lloyd started planning what he wanted to say Sunday. "I'm not sure I have anything to say to these people," he thought. "But it sure seems that they have a lot they want to say to each other." He selected a few readings that he thought would provide the most comfort and a couple of hymns they'd likely know from memory. Then he had an idea. "Trudy, do you think people would like a shared-dish potluck after worship on Sunday?"

"Well, I'll bet we all have thawed food we have to use up. We could cook on the gas stove at the church. Maybe a few people could bring their barbecue grills. But how will you get the word out to bring food?"

"I've been thinking about that. We'll call the members we can and add the potluck meal information to the posters at Emanuel. If we get power back by Saturday afternoon, we'll do an e-mail blast. We'll call it 'The Emanuel Mystery Buffet.'" They headed to bed—feeling as though breakfast that morning had been at least a week ago.

When Evelyn awoke Friday morning, she felt more tired than usual, and although she had agreed to take today off, she couldn't bring herself to do it. There was nothing to do at home, and there was much that needed to be done at church. As she prepared herself a breakfast of cereal and milk without her usual two cups of coffee, she remembered her resolve to do something for the security people working double shifts to help others.

Remembering the make-do coffee the Red Cross cooks had offered, she went to the basement to find some thermoses she had stored there. Finding three of them, she packed up her things and headed to the Emanuel kitchen to brew coffee for the rescue workers. Her plan was to be in and out before Lloyd arrived to remind her she was supposed to be off today.

She was just pouring coffee into the third thermos when Monica wandered into the kitchen. Evelyn was shocked to see her and thought she looked awful. Evelyn's first instinct was to say so, but she caught herself and asked, "What's happening with your family?"

Slowly Monica told the story: The Latrells had three feet of water in their home. Early Thursday morning they'd carried Danny and Benjamin out to the car but couldn't get out of the neighborhood because of the high water and a blocked driveway. They stayed on the second floor watching the water rise as rescue helicopters and boats came and went. Late in the afternoon, they gave up on being spotted by one of them and decided to try to walk out of the neighborhood. Monica and Wayne started trudging out on foot, each carrying a child. A state park ranger in a small aluminum boat saw the bedraggled family and picked them up. He gave them a ride to dry ground where they were—amazingly—delivered here to Emanuel and the Red Cross shelter.

"Our home away from home," she said. "Sleeping here last night was almost like being here at a junior-high lock-in. At least it was dry, and the emergency generators allowed for some light and fans. I thought maybe I could help out somehow."

Although Monica was trying to sound upbeat, Evelyn thought she looked a bit like a shell-shocked soldier coming into a medic's tent from the front lines. Evelyn held her for a long time and then led her back to the office.

Lloyd was already there. He forgot all about Evelyn's pledge to take the day off when he saw Monica's condition. He didn't know what to say or do. His conversation with Evelyn and Monica was interrupted by a visit from Clarence Goodyear, his denomination's district judicatory coordinator. Clarence's office was located in Yorkshire, and it had taken him twice as long as usual to make the trip over that morning. Clarence was spending his Friday checking up on the district's congregations and staff members located in the disaster area. Between the flooding Green River and the damage caused by the high winds, his visit covered nearly all of Green County.

Clarence figured that the staff would be feeling pretty much out of control and worried about many things—most of which they could do little or nothing about. It was only 9:30 A.M. Friday, a little over twenty-four hours since Lloyd and the others in Caldwell had first become aware how widespread the disaster was. Already Lloyd felt as if he'd been dealing with the aftermath of this disaster for a month or more.

He invited Clarence, Monica, Evelyn, and Faith Monroe, from the shelter, to join him for an impromptu meeting about the best use of staff time and Emanuel's space for the next few days. Obviously, there was need for a shelter. Monica's own family was proof of that. But there would also be a need for a safe daytime place for children to stay in the days to come. Parents would want help with their children, so they could begin to deal with their housing situation. The kids would need some stability and calm. Emanuel was fortunate to have great facilities that were designed to serve children. They were not suitably equipped for a long-term shelter, though—limited bathroom facilities, no showers; and privacy was a rare commodity.

While they were meeting, Jack Shaffer came in, hoping to find a cup of coffee. The FEMA voluntary agency liaison (VAL) for the area, he'd just arrived in town after an arduous four-hour road trip. He knew Emanuel was opening up today as a point-of-distribution (POD) site. He wanted to introduce himself and maybe track down a cup of coffee. He hadn't found any place open on his drive into town.

"Jack Shaffer here," he said, coming into Lloyd's cozy and crowded lantern-lit office. "With FEMA. I understand you're hosting one of our PODs. Thank you. The truck should be here shortly. We sure do appreciate you folks doing this."

"We're glad to be of help," Lloyd said. "Let me introduce you around. This is Pastor Clarence Goodyear, head of our conference area; Monica Latrell, our preschool director and at the moment an occupant of our Red Cross shelter; Evelyn Wright, the main 'go-to' person around here. If you need something, she's your best bet. And this is Faith Monroe, coordinating the Red Cross shelter for us."

Jack spent the next few minutes explaining how FEMA works in a disaster area. "Sometimes we're the agency that people most like to hate," he said with a sigh. "There are a lot of really good people trying to do an impossible task under impossible circumstances."

"How so?" asked Clarence. He'd already heard a lot of complaining and frustration about FEMA responses to other disasters at some of the national conferences he attended. He was glad to have a chance to meet someone from FEMA in person.

"Our main mission is to support the local governments as they rebuild whatever infrastructure was damaged by the disaster," Jack began. "It might mean providing funds to reopen roads or waterways. It might be getting communication and power stations open again. We try to reduce the negative impact of a disaster by providing things like these POD sites and assisting with temporary housing."

"Looks like we're going to need a lot of that around here," Monica said.

"There are a lot of challenges. We have many layers of decision makers to get through. The need is very local and well known to the people living through the disaster. The funds are usually far away, and it takes a lot of paperwork to release funds. I don't want to sound like I'm trying to make excuses. But we're a giant agency with many demands and thousands of people involved in the funding end of it all."

"This doesn't sound very encouraging," said Lloyd.

"A lot of really good people are trying to get the job done. I'm here to introduce myself and offer whatever assistance I can. And maybe find some coffee. Disaster staff run pretty much on adrenaline and caffeine."

Jack exchanged business cards with Clarence, Faith, and Lloyd. Faith offered to take him to the shelter area to get a cup of coffee. Jack promised to check back in later and followed Faith down the hall. (See appendix D for more information about FEMA's role in disaster-recovery work).

A Decision to Make

Should Emanuel reopen its preschool next week? Although Emanuel had excellent facilities, the area being used for the shelter operation included areas needed to operate the preschool. On top of that, at least four of the preschool staff members were dealing with their own problems stemming from the disaster. Monica and her family were flooded out of their home. So was another teacher. A couple of teachers had evacuated with their families.

Yet they knew there would be a need to provide safe, calm places to encourage children to tell what had happened to them and their families because of the storm. Also, part of the Emanuel DPR plan included using the church's well-run and highly respected preschool as a resource for community parents who would need to tend to many tasks following a disaster. This plan, of course, was based on the assumption that the congregation would have full use of the facilities.

Yes. The preschool was a much-needed resource.

- There were enough staff members and volunteer staff available to run the school if leaders did a little creative thinking about how to group the children in classes.
- The preschool part of the facilities came through the storm undamaged and was designed especially to meet the needs of young children.
- Children would need something familiar and stable to offset the emotional turmoil they and their families had experienced.
- Parents would need a safe place to leave younger children as they began the tedious task of assessing damage, mucking out their homes, and filling out the forms required to apply for disaster relief aid.

No. The people who would ordinarily run the school needed time to tend to their own families' needs.

- The power might not be back on yet, and it would be too challenging for the staff to try to care for the children without power.
- The facilities were too valuable as a Red Cross shelter, and people might still need the shelter next week.
- Although teachers and volunteers would no doubt rise to the challenge, most of them had their own disaster-related problems to worry about.

Maybe they could send in staff available to help and to meet Red Cross shelter needs.

- The Red Cross generally tried to empty out shelters as quickly as possible and might close by Sunday.
- Monica and others could put out a call for additional help on Sunday at worship and see if they could put together teams, so that staff people would have adequate time to tend to their own recovery needs in addition to helping provide for children.
- Reopening the preschool could be made contingent on having power restored to the facilities or locating sufficient generators to run at least lights and fans.

What You Need to Know about . . .

CONGREGATIONS' INITIAL RESCUE AND RELIEF EFFORTS

Although few congregations invest the time and energy to formulate a disaster-response plan, members and nonmembers alike generally turn to local congregations for comfort and assistance when a disaster disrupts their community. Most people hold church leaders in high regard and trust them to know what to do when everything seems crazy and unmanageable.

1. A 2001 national poll sponsored by the American Red Cross found that 59 percent of disaster victims said they preferred to talk to a spiritual counselor, compared to 45 percent who preferred a physician, and 40 percent a mental health professional. (The statistics are from an American Red Cross national poll conducted October 5–8, 2001, by Caravan ARC Intl., as reported in Kevin Massey, *Light Our Way: A Guide for Spiri-*

tual Care in Times of Disaster for Disaster Response Volunteers, First Responders and Disaster Planners (Arlington, Va.: National Voluntary Organizations Active in Disaster, 2006), ii.

2. Volunteers do not need to be trained counselors to provide much-needed assistance and spiritual first aid in a disaster area. The main requirements are a pair of listening ears, a compassionate heart, and willingness to be present in the midst of trauma.
3. The amount of outside assistance needed to help a community is proportional to the magnitude of the disaster. The needed help comes from a network of governmental agencies, nonprofit organizations, faith-based organizations, and individual volunteers drawn to disaster areas for a variety of personal reasons.
4. Over the years various organizations have developed their own areas of focus and methods of responding. All NGOs (nongovernmental organizations) depend on volunteers to deliver the services they provide. Well-intentioned but untrained volunteers can either help or hinder the relief efforts. To be effective, volunteers need these "Be attitudes":

   - Be flexible and patient as those in charge get the relief operations set up.
   - Be resourceful and knowledgeable about where and how to obtain appropriate local supplies and other resources.
   - Be calm in the presence of overwhelming tragedy and suffering.
   - Be able to let go of preconceived notions about how things "ought to work."
   - Be a student willing to learn rather than an expert wanting to teach.
   - Be willing to leave personal faith convictions at home and to focus on nonjudgmental listening.

5. Volunteers from faith-based groups need to understand that chaos is common in the first few days of a disaster. They can help communicate the latest information available, making sure not to make any promises they cannot keep.
6. Religious leaders play an important pre-disaster role by helping people prepare before disaster strikes. Then, when a disaster occurs, they can help their own members think of appropriate ways to respond, and they can encourage people to respond rather than react. Enabling people to take initiative in their own recovery plans helps the whole network of responders work more effectively.

Implications for Your Congregation

Should a disaster occur in your community, congregational leaders will be pulled in several directions. A disaster preparation and response plan can help leaders decide how to make best use of limited time, energy, and resources. (See appendix E for a sample congregational disaster plan.)

1. Everyone who lives in a disaster zone is affected in some way—but not equally. Some lose everything they had—home, cars, priceless family heirlooms, tools of their trade. Others may be inconvenienced but lose very little. Some may have loved ones die in the disaster, or soon after from stress. Some develop health problems after a disaster. People suffer differing levels of emotional, mental, and spiritual stress and are certainly affected personally in some way. Religious leaders will have to juggle their own needs with those of their families and the people they lead.
2. Few congregational leaders have been trained in advance of a disaster for response work. They will therefore be going through their own recovery process while learning how to

help others in their community recover. They will likely feel enormous responsibility and concern for the members of their congregation but may not know how best to provide aid and comfort to others who are struggling.

3. Congregational leaders are often drawn to "helper" roles. In a disaster, they may feel both called and obligated to be "out there" doing something to respond. Yet the more they respond to this sense of call, the more difficult it will be to maintain the ongoing day-to-day ministries of the congregation. Facing these competing needs and agendas can cause even more stress for leaders.

Victim? Survivor? Rescue Worker?

In the weeks and months after Hurricane Katrina in New Orleans, religious leaders often described themselves as patients who were asked to be the doctors. Anne Burkholder of the Florida Conference of the United Methodist Church reported that of the thirteen clergy serving twelve churches most affected by Hurricane Andrew in 1992, all but two experienced long-term negative consequences. Three took early retirement; four suffered serious illness (one of these died); three experienced serious emotional problems; two were divorced; and three left the pastoral ministry (Kevin Massey, *Light Our Way: A Guide for Spiritual Care in Times of Disaster for Disaster Response Volunteers, First Responders and Disaster Planners* (Arlington, Va.: National Voluntary Organizations Active in Disaster, 2006, 40–41).

4. It is common for faith-based leaders to overfunction following a disaster. There are a myriad of tragic situations and unmet needs to address. For those used to putting the needs of others ahead of their own needs, it is difficult to take adequate time for rest, recreation, and relaxation.
5. The community will find itself hosting strangers from all over the country. They come on behalf of disaster-response

organizations, utility and construction companies, insurance companies, and other organizations involved in rescue, cleanup, and recovery work. Religious communities that take seriously the ministry of hospitality can have a huge positive impact on the recovery process by extending a welcome mat to these out-of-town visitors.

Resource

Future with Hope, *www.futurewithhope.org*. A website developed by the Gulf Coast Synod of the Evangelical Lutheran Church in America following hurricanes Katrina and Rita.

Questions for Reflection

1. How do you respond when faced with competing expectations and needs?
2. How do you decide which thing to do when you experience a conflict of time or commitment?
3. What helps you calm down when your life is stressful?
4. Have you put together a family emergency kit? If so, what's in your kit? If not, what would help you get one put together?
5. How could disaster recovery ministry fit in with other mission goals of your congregation?

Scripture Reflection

We always thank God for all of you, mentioning you in our prayers. We continually remember before our God and Father your work produced by faith, your labor prompted by love, and your endurance inspired by hope in our LORD Jesus Christ.

—1 Thessalonians 1:2–3

CHAPTER 6

People, People Everywhere

NATIONAL RESPONSE ORGANIZATIONS

Send forth your light and your truth,
let them guide me;
let them bring me to your holy mountain,
to the place where you dwell.
—Psalm 43:3

Timeline

Later Friday. The rescue and initial relief efforts continue. Government-affiliated rescue workers are visible everywhere in the community. Representatives of various nongovernmental organizations begin to appear on the scene. Conversations are changing from rescue efforts to short-term relief efforts. The staff and lead volunteers of Emanuel decide to reopen the preschool midweek the following week.

Situation

During their impromptu meeting about whether to focus on reopening the preschool or continuing to serve as a Red Cross shelter, the Emanuel leaders decided they could do more to help the community if they reopened their preschool as soon as possible. As a result, the Red Cross staff announced it would start helping shelter residents make other arrangements and close the shelter next Tuesday after lunch. This change would enable Emanuel members to open the preschool on Wednesday. The decision was to be announced at lunch on Friday, giving residents four days to plan for their next step.

FEMA representatives were already taking applications for assistance and committing to pay for motel rooms for the next thirty days. The problem was that no motel rooms were available within an hour's drive of Caldwell. Those not occupied by people forced out of their homes by the flood were housing various rescue and relief workers serving the area—or were too damaged to be used for the time being. Insurance adjusters and building contractors were also competing for motel rooms.

Of course, nothing was normal at the moment, and options were limited, but the Red Cross staff was committed to getting people into alternative housing. They were setting up a mass tent shelter at the county fairgrounds. While living in a tent was not an attractive option, it was better than nothing. "Too many people have a whole lot of nothing right now," Faith sighed as they wrapped up the meeting between Emanuel staff and Red Cross staff.

Monica said she and her family would stay with friends in Yorkshire for the time being. From there, she felt confident she could help find enough staff to take care of the children. Monica and the preschool board wanted to open the Emanuel preschool to any residents of the community needing assistance with their children during this chaotic time. They'd ask for volunteer donations to cover the cost and figure out the financial details later. Perhaps the preschool would qualify for some kind of "loss of revenue" compensation from its insurance. It was a possibility worth looking into.

Lloyd volunteered that until Trudy's school reopened, Trudy would have time to assist—and could pull in some community resources to help provide mental-health care for the children. Although she hadn't seen the school for herself yet, her principal had called to say that it would be closed for at least two weeks because of wind and water damage. Part of the roof blew off in the high winds, and the school lost most of its office equipment. Also, a couple of classrooms sustained water damage.

Clarence Goodyear reminded Monica to screen any volunteers who weren't already part of the regular paid or volunteer staff. "Can't be too careful who you let work with other people's children—especially now when everyone's a bit jittery. Those with less-than-honorable intentions look for such moments of vulnerability to get access to the kids."

Monica said she'd solicit volunteers from among Emanuel's own members and some of the other preschool and Mothers' Day Out programs in town. Her parents' congregation also ran a large preschool program; perhaps some of its staff could help out.

Since it was late morning by the time the meeting ended, Lloyd sent Evelyn to see whether there was room for a few more people around the Red Cross lunch table. Evelyn and Lloyd ate a quick lunch of soup and sandwiches, then spread out to visit with the various shelter residents to hear their stories. They wanted to be available to support those who might be most upset to learn the shelter would be closing in a few days.

In between talking with various drop-in guests, Lloyd worked out details for the service on Sunday. In a moment of inspiration he remembered that Hal Beckman now worked at the Green County Hospital. Surely the hospital had generator power sufficient to run office equipment. He called Hal to see if his hunch was correct. When Lloyd explained that if at all possible, he wanted printed materials to give participants on Sunday, Hal said he couldn't help. "We do have generators—but we use them only to run critical equipment. I don't think I could persuade anyone that printed bulletins for a church service met that criteria."

"I understand," Lloyd said. "Of course, we don't want to endanger someone's life just so we can have the words to our favorite hymns. I just thought it'd be nice to send people home with something to use after Sunday."

"Great idea. Tell you what. I'll drive over to Yorkshire tomorrow and get the bulletins run off at a quick-print shop. Are you carving them on stone tablets, or do you have a battery-powered laptop?"

"Evelyn to the rescue again. She dug out a very old manual typewriter. It's about as fast as etching on stone—but a lot neater."

That worry crossed off his list, Lloyd carefully wrote out the worship notes and words to two favorite hymns by hand and left them for Evelyn to type. As he did so, he realized that if he'd had a backup battery for his laptop, he could have produced the bulletin on his computer. Even if he couldn't print it out or e-mail the file, he might have been able just to hand Hal a flash drive with the bulletin already done. "Oh well," he sighed. "Another hour, another learning curve for next time." He intentionally kept the service simple but included enough elements of a "normal" service to be familiar to the regulars. He also wanted to allow plenty of time for worshipers to tell their stories. If only a few people showed up, they could operate as one group. If more showed up, they could divide into smaller groups. He wanted to give everyone a chance to talk.

After he finished his notes for Evelyn, Lloyd decided the best use of his time for the remainder of the day was what he called the MBWA plan—Management by Wandering Around. The first person he came upon that Friday afternoon was Jack, the VAL from FEMA. Jack was looking for Lloyd to thank him again for letting FEMA use the Emanuel parking lot as an additional point of distribution. He was also wondering if Emanuel could provide volunteers to assist the FEMA staff people. They needed help directing traffic and loading supplies into people's cars or carts or wagons or whatever they brought with them to collect their ice and supply of MREs ("meals ready to eat"). Lloyd agreed to try to round up a few volunteers and told Jack that Emanuel would be hosting worship on Sunday. They worked out a plan to have the FEMA staff help direct worship traffic on Sunday.

Although Jack hadn't been inside a place of worship since his grandmother took him as a young child, he was pleased with the level of cooperation he was witnessing between his government agency and this faith community. He decided he might give the "God thing" another try when he got a chance.

Lloyd went back to the office to confirm that Evelyn had been able to reach Peg. "Did you tell her we have a job for her now and to be careful what she prays for?" he asked. Evelyn said she had reached Peg, who was thrilled to get involved in the effort to distribute food and ice to people.

The next person Lloyd came upon was his colleague Suzanne Winters, pastor of the congregation two blocks down the street. She thought a couple of her members were at the shelter. She and Lloyd compared notes about the storm. They decided it would be a good idea to call for a prayer breakfast for area clergy tomorrow. "We need each other right now," she said. "And what if we try to host a community service next Wednesday evening? That'll be the one-week anniversary of the storm." Lloyd nodded and told her he'd been thinking along the same lines but wasn't sure how to start to organize something.

They agreed that the storm was bringing out both the best and the worst behavior people had to offer. They were grateful for those people who quietly and calmly pitched in and did whatever needed to be done next. The list of little deeds of kindness ranged from offering many drinks of water to many shelter residents, to helping people fill out FEMA assistance forms, to comforting an upset toddler, to stirring the pot of soup that would become the next meal for hungry people.

Their conversation turned to storm damage at their respective buildings. They shared ideas on where to find a reputable firm to do the work, how to finance the expenses not covered by insurance, and how to function amid storm damage that seemed insurmountable. They also worried about the economic reality that offerings would surely go down just at a time when they would have more expenses than ever, between the damage to their facilities and the needs of people all around them.

Knowing that he and his colleagues were in for a long, difficult path ahead, Lloyd agreed to get in touch with a few others to let them know about the breakfast. Only a few restaurants in the community were open, but one of his favorite coffee shops was among them. They'd gather there at eight the next morning. Lloyd said he would also bring a couple of his DPR team members. Suzanne thanked him: "This storm's convinced me that every congregation ought to have such a group. You can teach us how to get them going."

Lloyd went to Evelyn's desk to call a couple of DPR team members to invite them. He was looking up Sammy Ellison's number when Sammy called him. "Hey, Sammy! I was getting ready to call you. How's it going out there?" Sammy had promised to help get supplies and some volunteers to do the temporary repair work at Emanuel.

Now he was apologizing that he couldn't get to it for a while. Normally he worked as a part-time medic a few days a month. But since the storm, he was working long days helping county officials search houses in the flood area. They were looking for people who were stranded—or worse, who hadn't lived through the storm. Lloyd knew Sammy had found a few who didn't make it out alive. Although Sammy had been brief and vague about details, Lloyd sensed from the tone of Sammy's voice that he really wanted to talk. Like many rescue workers who take on the toughest assignments in disasters, he didn't want to admit that he could use some emotional support. After letting Sammy talk for a few minutes, Lloyd assured him that others could help with the church repairs, but there weren't many who had what it took to do what Sammy was doing.

Next Lloyd took a walk around the building. A line at least the length of three football fields snaked through the parking lot and down the street as people waited their turn for FEMA supplies. Lloyd noted that most of them were waiting patiently. Others were clearly agitated and angry. His heart went out to all of them, especially the workers who couldn't keep up. The more people they served, the longer the lines seemed to grow. Seeing people lined up to receive their modest supply of food, water, and ice reminded him of the long bread lines he'd seen in documentaries from the Great Depression. "We surely are on the brink of some kind of a depression around here," he thought as he headed back to his office.

He nodded at Evelyn, who was hard at work trying to decipher his handwriting. He went into his office and closed the door. He had nothing further to say to God at the moment, but he desperately needed a quiet moment to focus on whatever God might have to say to him. "Dear God, be present in this place and God help us all," he prayed finally.

When he went back to Evelyn, she handed him a message from Lillian Yeager, the regional representative of his denomination's disaster-response organization. "She said it was urgent and asked if you could call her sometime today—even if it's late tonight."

Lloyd sighed and picked up the phone. Lillian said her agency was looking for some office space to start setting up a response effort in the area. It wouldn't cost Emanuel anything. In fact, the organization was prepared to compensate the congregation for use of the facilities, including a portion of utility expenses. She'd gotten a recommendation to call him from Clarence Goodyear. Her agency was also exploring the need for a camp where out-of-town response volunteers could stay in the area—perhaps using tents or trailers in the church parking lot, or space in a fellowship hall or Sunday-school rooms. "Do you think your church might consider something like this?"

"How soon do you need to know?"

"We were hoping to have someone on site by next week. As you know, there's an awful lot of work to do. We're already getting calls from churches as far away as Colorado wanting to know when they can send in volunteers to help us. We don't want them in here just yet—but we sure don't want to alienate them either. We need to get someone in the area as soon as possible to assess the needs and determine how best to support the volunteers who will do the bulk of the recovery work."

"OK. Can I sleep on it? We're already running a shelter, and we just decided to reopen our preschool next week. Would this mean we have to close our preschool?"

"No," said Lillian, we've often run volunteers camps at churches with preschools. The volunteers are out for the day before the kids arrive and don't come back from the work site until long after the kids leave leave. It means a little extra work putting things away and getting them out every day—but we have volunteers to do that. It's part of the plan for them when they come into the area.

"Of course, you need time to think it over," she added. "You must be getting pretty run down with all this activity and all the decisions being thrown at you and your folks. One thing—if you are able to do this—a disaster chaplain will be available to you and any of your staff and members. Chaplains come with the package. They come and go; they're volunteers too. Most stay a week or two. We'll also send in a computer whiz who will set up a database to track all the volunteers we're expecting in the months to come. We may also need to hire some additional staff to coordinate the effort."

Lloyd started to feel completely overwhelmed by the many decisions, the chaos, the never-ending stories of loss and tragedy, and his own lack of adequate sleep and food. He'd never thought about just how all-consuming a disaster could be. Lloyd told Lillian that he'd think about her request and talk it over with a few folks. "I'll try to get back to you early next week."

A Decision to Make

Should Emanuel consider working with its denomination's national disaster-response organization (DRO) to provide office space for staff and possible housing for volunteers?

Yes. The need is great, and Emanuel must respond.

- The congregation had the facilities and clearly could see the need.
- Emanuel's own DPR team had already expressed a willingness to help with day-to-day details and recruit the necessary people and resources.
- Doing it would not only help the congregation's own members, but also make it possible for Emanuel to make a significant contribution to the recovery effort of the region.

- With a little patience, creative thinking, and trial-and-error efforts, the staff should be able to run the preschool and meet the DRO's space needs.

No. The congregation's doing all it can do.

- Who would feed all those people?
- Who would do all that laundry?
- There were no shower facilities.
- People wanted to get back to normal as soon as possible. This step would delay that for many months—maybe even years.

Maybe Emanuel could do something.

- There was clearly a need. If the logistics were clearly spelled out with the disaster-response staff ahead of time, so that Emanuel members understood why the church was providing space and how it would work, it might be manageable.
- This effort could give the church a chance to partner with other congregations and facilities in the neighborhood that did have shower facilities.
- Emanuel could try it on a sixty-day trial basis and then re-evaluate.

What You Need to Know about . . .

NATIONAL DISASTER RESPONSE ORGANIZATIONS

Once local and state governments call on the federal government to declare a federal disaster area, a predetermined plan of action begins to unfold. First, National Guard troops and other governmental organizations arrive to assist local law-enforcement and emergency personnel with search-and-rescue operations. A variety of entities are engaged in this immediate response, such as law-enforcement personnel, firefighters, emergency medical technicians, and national, state, and county parks-and-wildlife staffs.

1. While these first responders do their work, the Red Cross is establishing short-term shelters and working with local governmental and nonprofit organizations to find more substantial transitional housing for people whose homes have sustained too much damage for them to be allowed to return. Some of this housing will be FEMA trailers like those that became "home" to some people for years following hurricanes Katrina and Rita. Meanwhile, FEMA is moving in to establish points of distribution (PODs).
2. Most religious denominations also have national disaster-response organizations that will send staff to do an assessment of any facilities and professional staff affiliated with that denomination. These initial visits usually occur any time from a few days to a few weeks after the disaster. The timing of the first-assessment visits depends on how soon it is safe to enter a disaster area. Judicatory leaders generally also have some system in place to determine the status of their clergy and lay staffs as soon as possible.
3. Some members of Voluntary Organizations Active in Disaster (VOAD) are part of this initial humanitarian relief effort. For example, the Southern Baptist Convention's men's group generally brings in portable kitchens.
4. The role of the first responders is to rescue people and provide the basic resources needed to sustain life—food, water, and shelter. Their goal is to save lives; they do not focus on trying to make life comfortable or on addressing secondary, long-term recovery issues.
5. Most national religious relief organizations such as Lutheran Disaster Response, the United Methodist Committee on Relief, Presbyterian Disaster Response, United Jewish Commu-

nities, and Catholic Charities are not first responders. They generally begin to move into a disaster area as first responders are completing their work and winding down. These national teams work with local affiliates and officials to set up a long-term recovery process.

6. Volunteers who travel away from home to help in a disaster area must realize that they will encounter people of backgrounds and beliefs very different from their own. Differences will manifest themselves in what particular cultures consider appropriate and inappropriate ways to express grief; the proper way to honor and bury the dead; willingness or resistance to accepting professional help for emotional trauma; foods that offer comfort; and appropriate religious rituals.
7. First responders often risk their own lives in their efforts to save others—usually total strangers. However, they cannot possibly address all the problems that will emerge after a disaster. First responders also require attention, appreciation, and help working through what they've seen and dealt with in the midst of the disaster.

Partners in Disaster Response Ministry

Virtually every type of faith-based organization with a national structure has a national disaster-response agency. Most of these agencies belong to National Voluntary Organizations Active in Disaster (NVOAD). Each of the fifty states has a state VOAD chapter and often many regional and local VOADs. A great deal of disaster-recovery work is accomplished by this network.

Communities located in areas more likely to experience recurring disasters from flooding, hurricanes, winter storms, or earthquakes may have VOAD organizations permanently in place. These VOAD groups may be dormant during non-disaster periods, meeting only occasionally for networking and information sharing. Recently a movement has been underway to use the calm times for disaster-preparedness education in the community. VOAD groups

> quickly expand both in number of participants and frequency of meetings when a disaster occurs and during the long recovery phase afterward.
>
> A local VOAD group is an excellent place to start learning more about how to do volunteer work in a disaster area. See appendix E for a complete list of members.

Implications for Your Congregation

Typically congregations in a disaster area struggle with the tension between trying to resume pre-disaster programming and ministries and being a visible and active partner in the community's ongoing recovery work.

1. Sooner or later a congregation must return to functioning as a worshiping community that focuses on its pre-disaster ministries.
2. No one congregation can or should meet all the needs that will surface. Disasters provide a great opportunity to meet and partner with ecumenical neighbors. The best time to do this is before there is a disaster. However, cooperation after the disaster opens many doors to provide the most effective local faith-based response to the disaster.
3. Congregations often make important connections with volunteers from companion congregations of their denomination who travel from afar to help with the recovery effort. These connections can become a major part of the recovery process as these volunteers go home to make the case for financial support and more volunteers. These volunteers might then invite people from the disaster area to visit their hometowns to tell the story. This exchange strengthens the network between congregations and provides some much-needed change of scenery for people affected by disasters.
4. Congregations that host out-of-town volunteers help infuse new energy into the congregations sending the volunteers.

Disaster-response ministry ultimately blesses those who lend a helping hand as much as it helps the disaster victims. Disaster volunteers often go home to report that their time spent "mucking out" flooded homes or helping rebuild was the most rewarding experience of their life.

5. When congregations embrace the many challenges of disaster-recovery work, they often find that they themselves experience an exciting renewal of mission and sense of purpose. Disaster-response work grabs hold of people's passions and deepens their faith in ways that often surprise both those who help and those who receive the help.
6. Funding quickly becomes a major factor in disaster-recovery work. The more people a congregation can help host for the disaster-recovery work, the more "missionaries" there will be reporting about the ongoing need to their home congregations. Even the largest disasters fade from the public limelight long before the recovery work is completed. Keeping the story alive is an important part of securing the resources needed for the long-term disaster recovery process.

Resource

National Voluntary Organizations Active in Disaster, *www.nvoad.org*

Questions for Reflection

1. Describe some of your volunteer work. What worked out well for you? What do you wish had gone differently?
2. If you needed help repairing your home after a flood or fire, what would you want a volunteer to know before he or she offered to help you?
3. What's the longest period of time you could be away from home in a makeshift housing situation and not start to feel deprived?

4. How often do you think someone working in disaster relief ministry should take a day off?
5. What would your congregation be like if it were suddenly to be the site for a new set of volunteer guests every week?
6. Can you think of members who would be excited about the opportunity to get involved in disaster-response ministry by serving meals, preparing places for people to stay, offering up their own homes for out-of-town visitors from various agencies, or doing hands-on work to help clean up and do reconstruction work?
7. Does your congregation have a savings account or endowment fund for a rainy day? If not, could you start one? If you do have one, are there clear policies on what would constitute a rainy day? Who decides when and how these funds are used?

Scripture Reflection

Hear this, all you peoples;
listen, all who live in this world,
both low and high,
rich and poor alike:
My mouth will speak words of wisdom;
the utterance from my heart will give understanding
—Psalm 49: 1–3

CHAPTER 7

Bring in the Volunteers

GOVERNMENT AND NONGOVERNMENTAL AGENCY ROLES IN DISASTER

Peace I leave with you, my peace I give you.
I do not give to you as the world gives.
Do not let your hearts be troubled and do not be afraid.
—John 14:27

Timeline

Saturday and Sunday. People are still in shelters and learning that they likely will be in transitional housing for weeks, if not months. Red Cross personnel and staff from other nonprofit organizations are gearing up to find more suitable housing for those who cannot return home. FEMA is still distributing emergency supplies and is now also taking applications for financial assistance. Insurance adjusters have come in from across the country. The members of Emanuel have decided they do not want to use the church space for a volunteer camp, but that Emanuel can provide office space and support to the agency staff people as they are getting organized.

Situation

The clergy breakfast meeting lasted all the way to lunch. Twenty-two area religious leaders and lay leaders came, and all had stories to add to the unfolding drama about what happened as a result of the storm. They all agreed they needed a community ecumenical service and that Wednesday evening would be the most appropriate time to hold it. When they got stuck on where to hold it, Jill Hanson, chair of the Emanuel DPR team, suggested they see if the auditorium at the Green County Hospital would be available. "We're all hurting and need of healing. And the hospital has a large neutral place to gather. Seems like a natural location." After more discussion the leaders agreed that it was a good idea if they could make it work. Hal Beckman and three others volunteered to work out details and get back to the rest of them on Monday or Tuesday. Hal said he'd see about using the hospital auditorium right away.

Can't We All Just Get Along?

Identifying an appropriately neutral community-worship site is an important part of planning a post-disaster religious event. Worship planners need to honor diverse religious points of view and avoid unintentionally offending each other. Those who are uncomfortable with traditions radically different from their own would do well to respectfully decline attending rather than going and being critical of how the event is put together.

Let the focus be on creating a safe public space for trauma victims to talk about what has happened to them. After a disaster, even highly diverse people share the common experience of loss and trauma. Although not all individuals will suffer the same level of loss in a disaster, everyone living in or near a disaster zone will be affected in any number of ways. Everything will change. Traffic will be difficult when lights are out and emergency responders and catastrophic units of insurance companies move in. Schools may shut down for a while. Businesses may have to close. Hospitals may have to run on limited staff or close until damage is repaired. Fresh supplies of groceries may be limited or unavailable. Extra security may be in evidence in public places. Some roads may be closed. Every aspect of daily life is altered in some way after a disaster. People usually experience healing and strength being with others who have experienced the same situation. A public worship service is one way to acknowledge the effects of the disaster on the entire community.

Individual worship communities should also gather members together, helping people to grieve and console one another using familiar religious rituals. When a whole community is hurting, both public and private events are needed.

> *This is a time for compassion and presence, not a time for conviction and recruitment of new members. Public memorial services in a disaster area often combine both the faith community and the power structure of the community. There can be a tension between the need for privacy on the part of families who have suffered great losses and the need of a curious public that wants to be included and allowed to show their concern and support.*
>
> *There is much room for beauty and grace. There is also much room for insensitivity and outrage.*
>
> —Earl E. Johnson
> Coordinator of Spiritual Care Response Team
> American Red Cross

After lunch Lloyd, Jill, and Hal decided to drive through the parts of town they could reach. They wanted to see how extensive the damage to their community was and who was already at work helping with the massive cleanup effort. They also wanted a little time together to debate the merits and potential problems of letting their denominational disaster-response organization use Emanuel as a volunteer housing site.

Many parts of Caldwell were still closed off to everyone except officials. The trio found that many first responders were suspicious of them, even when they introduced themselves as being from Emanuel and part of the congregation's DPR team. Lloyd, Jill, and Hal tried to persuade the people at checkpoints that all they wanted to know was "How are you doing?" and "How can we help you?" But though the storm had occurred less than a week earlier, some self-appointed heroes had already shown up, eager to help. A few of the first responders had stories to tell about overzealous, religion-affiliated, early-bird volunteers who practically assaulted the people they claimed to be helping. Other unsolicited volunteers were inadequately prepared to take care of themselves around toxic and unstable areas. They sometimes unknowingly put their own health at risk. Experienced disaster-relief professionals knew how quickly a situation could get even worse when untrained and uninvited volunteers arrived with little understanding of how to be helpful.

Once the Emanuel folk convinced the first responders that they were local, willing to learn, and genuinely concerned about how the out-of-town responders were doing, one man with a crew from New York started talking. He said their chaplain came with them and needed a quiet place for rescue workers to rest when they got off work. He wondered if Emanuel had a place that could be used for that. Lloyd, Jill, and Hal talked it over briefly and quickly agreed that they could set up the adult forum classroom for that purpose. It was quiet, undamaged by the storm, and away from the busyness of the rest of the church; and it had its own bathroom facilities. Lloyd handed the New York crew leader his business card and told him to call anytime to get started.

Not All Help Is Helpful

Real help is about the victims, not the volunteers. Volunteers are central to disaster recovery. However, it's important that they understand their role in recovery and accept their limitations. Appendix F provides tips on things to know before you go into a disaster area as a volunteer. For example, volunteers need to understand that the more local residents can do for themselves and their neighbors, the smoother their disaster-recovery process will be. Although large-scale disasters depend on large numbers of volunteers to get the job of recovery done, the final responsibility for recovery belongs with the people living where the disaster occurred.

So on the one hand, disaster-recovery volunteers are the lifeblood of the recovery process. On the other hand, volunteers who show up without adequate training or understanding of how the process typically unfolds can add stress to an already stressful situation. This distinction is especially the case with independent volunteers who show up on their own, without any affiliation or the blessing of an organized disaster-response agency.

There is a significant difference, for example, between a volunteer's taking out a chainsaw and clearing the neighborhood around his home and a volunteer's getting in a car and driving across the state or the country expecting to be part of an impromptu cleanup crew. Volunteers who show up on their own, expecting to be fed, housed, assigned, supported, and in some way thanked, are yet another challenge for already overtaxed disaster-response workers to manage.

Disaster-recovery ministry is humanitarian aid at the most basic level. The people of a devastated area are in desperate circumstances through factors beyond their control. The goals of volunteering in a disaster zone should be (1) to do whatever enables people to begin providing for themselves as soon as possible and (2) to refrain from doing anything that impedes achieving that aim. Effective volunteers work through one of the dozens of disaster response organizations. *Disaster response ministry is NOT about the volunteer's need to be needed.*

Their first look at the areas most devastated by the combination of high water and strong winds startled them all. Hearing about the damage from the news and first-person reports didn't prepare them for how extensive the damage was. One of the rescue workers told them to walk up to the top of a hill that overlooked the slowly receding Green River. From there they saw mud, piles of debris, and an odd assortment of common household furnishings strewn as far as they could see. Clothing hung from tree branches. Many trees lay toppled onto one another or onto the roofs of homes. Some houses were still islands of brick, stone, or wood in the middle of the swollen river. Some were missing an outside wall or had large holes that exposed the contents of the room inside.

Hal had seen a scene like this before in New Orleans, but he never thought he'd have to witness it again. He was visibly upset—too upset to speak. Lloyd tried to talk but realized he really had nothing useful to say. Jill stood silently with large tears running down her cheeks. It seemed disrespectful to talk in the midst of such destruction. But then their silence became unbearable. "I don't see how we can *not* do something to help house some volunteers after seeing this," said Jill.

"I know," Hal agreed. "But do our own people have the energy to take in volunteers?"

"I suggest we put that question to them tomorrow at the service," said Lloyd. "We don't have to get back to the national staff for a while yet. Let's sleep on it, pray about it tomorrow, and see what our people think. Maybe we can help in some other way that doesn't stretch our people too far." They walked in respectful and reflective silence the five minutes back to their car. They waved at the rescue worker who'd let them pass the yellow tape and didn't speak until they were back in the Emanuel neighborhood.

Back in Lloyd's office they discussed the best way to implement the congregation's DPR plan. Hal said he'd go home and reactivate the VC community calls, now that it seemed most people had figured out how to access phone service one way or another. He said he'd try to create a list by tomorrow morning of members who would need support for the long haul. While the VC coordinators were making their calls, he'd go over to Yorkshire to run the bulletins for tomorrow that Evelyn had left for him in her office. And, as promised, he would check with the director of the hospital about using the hospital auditorium.

Jill suggested they take stock of the basic supplies Emanuel members had been collecting as part of the church's disaster preparations.

Then they could put together care packages for any Emanuel families who were flooded out. Lloyd suggested that she put Cindy to work on that project. They were already starting to get calls from people wanting to donate everything from Beanie Babies to baseball equipment to used worship supplies. What was really needed were flood buckets, clean bedding, canned food, and cash. Lots and lots of cash.

Start with the Basics

Different disasters require different resources. Flood buckets are useful in areas where residents have to "muck out" their homes. They include disinfecting supplies, gloves, masks, scrub brushes, mops, cleaning rags, trash bags, and other items needed for the task. Also, because anything made even partly of cloth can absorb mold even if it didn't get wet from flood water, it has to be thrown out. If it can't fit into a washing machine, it goes to the curb. Clean bedding is one crucial need people will have.

Gift cards for stores that sell basic household items and building supplies are always popular in a disaster zone. Ask if there is a need for used clothing and other items before you send them. Storing items requires finding a suitable facility, trucks to move items around, and people to load and unload the donated goods.

Then they circled back to their discussion about what it might be like for Emanuel to be a volunteer center. How long would the volunteers be there? Who would feed them? What about the absence of shower facilities? "All questions we can't answer right now," Lloyd said. "I suspect all those questions have answers. We just don't know them yet." Jill and Hal admitted they'd never known that their own denomination had a national disaster-response organization before they started working on the Emanuel DPR Plan. "Why don't we hear more about this?" Jill asked.

"I guess because they work mostly behind the scenes and only in disaster areas. If you're not having a disaster, how much attention do you pay to disaster-recovery work? The humanitarian disaster folks have been around for a long time. We've just been fortunate enough not to need their kind of help until now."

"Well, we need to do more to educate ourselves and our people," said Hal.

"I agree," said Lloyd. "After we survive the next few weeks. For now, let's focus on gathering our folks together tomorrow and see how it goes. I don't know about you, but I'm already exhausted from everything that's happened in the past few days. Let's all call it quits and regroup tomorrow."

Hal took off to do his errands. Jill and Lloyd returned to their homes to spend a more-or-less quiet Saturday evening—still without power but grateful for a calm, quiet place to retreat from the stories, sights, sounds, and smells of the storm for a few hours.

Sunday brought a beautiful early fall morning. Evelyn looked out her kitchen window to see fluffy white clouds against a pale blue sky and the wind gently fluttering the leaves. "It's hard to believe that just a few days ago we were in the middle of one of the worst storms ever to come through these parts," she thought as she dined on her granola bars and the last hardboiled egg. A few minutes later she was on her way to Emanuel to help welcome whoever would show up for worship that morning.

By the time she arrived—an hour before the start of worship—there were already two dozen or more people gathered in the parking lot. The FEMA trailer was still the main focal point of the parking area. Workers wearing FEMA golf shirts greeted every car to direct the churchgoers one way and residents in search of FEMA supplies another. The side yard of the church was starting to look like the community park on the Fourth of July—only now the community park itself was a mound of mud, misplaced household goods, and torn-up trees. Because the park was still closed to the public, most Caldwell residents did not yet know how bad the damage was.

What people did know was that they wanted to try to make sense of the past four days and support one another in any way they could. The early arrivals had lined up lawn chairs in neat rows. Children played further out on the lawn. People arranged their contributions for lunch on long tables along one side of the church. It all looked organized and calm, as though they'd been worshiping this way for years.

Lloyd was in his office going over his notes by the light of his trusty lantern and a little light coming through the window. Evelyn poked her head in to say "Hi" and see how he was doing.

"Shall I invite the Red Cross shelter guests?" she asked.

"Already did. I put up a few signs. That way those who want to join us can, and those who don't won't feel obligated just because I asked them."

"Need anything?"

"Electricity would be nice."

"I'll see what I can do. Anything else?"

"Coffee?"

"Coming up." She headed to the kitchen to see if any was left from the shelter breakfast, or if she could figure out how to make just a couple of cups apiece for herself, Lloyd, and Trudy. As Evelyn was walking into the kitchen, the lights overhead began to flicker. They went on and off a few times and then—miracle of miracles—they stayed on. She raced back to the office. There she found Lloyd playing with the office light switch like a kid finally able to reach the switch for himself. He was grinning triumphantly at the prospect of having power again.

"There's not much about a disaster to recommend one to anyone," he said. "But a disaster does have a way of making us rethink our priorities and let go of an awful lot of things we worry about that aren't worth worrying about."

"Like electricity?"

"Like the fact that we are privileged to have it and seldom stop to realize that most people in the world don't—or have it only sporadically. Or that if we still have our health and our loved ones and enough to eat and a place to sleep, we're doing pretty good. We need each other. Maybe disasters help us know that more clearly."

"Sounds like a sermon theme to me."

"I think you're right. I've been working for two days now on what to say to our people this morning. I think I just said it. Thanks."

"You're welcome."

The rest of the morning went by in a blur as people gathered to draw support and encouragement from one another. Typical worship attendance for Emanuel was 360 over two morning services. This Sunday was anything but typical. People were gathering in the parking lot under a tent borrowed from a funeral home. The ushers guessed the attendance was over two hundred. Many of the faces were familiar. However, quite a few were first-time worshipers. The congregation included a few cautious Red Cross shelter residents, a few of the first responders still in town, a couple of FEMA volunteers, and at least a dozen employees of various stores where the congregation did business. "Disasters draw people together in new ways," Lloyd thought as he observed the people gathering before him.

After a few brief introductory thoughts to start the sermon time, Lloyd divided the people into groups of ten to twelve each and encouraged them to tell each other their stories. It was a half-hour before he was able to call them back together. When he finally had their attention, he offered up the prayers for the day.

When it came time for the offering, he asked a few people to pass out slips of paper and pencils. As they were doing that, he asked the worshipers to consider how they could best help a neighbor or friend in need of assistance. He said the ushers would pass the plate as usual. "However, I know most of you don't know what financial impact this storm will have for you. It's the same for our church. We'll be finding that out in the days and weeks to come. What we do know right now is that hundreds of people in our community need help. I believe God is counting on each of us to be part of the help they need. For our offering this morning, let's focus on what we can do to help one another. We will offer our ideas to God as our morning sacrifice. Then we'll watch how God uses our offerings."

He then told the people that the denomination's national disaster-response organization had asked if Emanuel would consider hosting volunteers. We can expect hundreds of volunteers to come to Caldwell in the weeks and months to come. They'll need a place to call home. It's a big decision for us, but it sure would help if we had a sense of what you're thinking. So please write down your thoughts on the back of that slip of paper. If you'd like, you can just jot down "yes," "no," or "maybe." However, we also welcome your comments."

After the offering was received, Lloyd read a few psalms and led the worshipers in a closing hymn. The worship service was greatly appreciated, if one could judge by the comments at the potluck. People needed to be together. They needed to tell their stories. They needed the ritual of worship, songs, Scripture readings, and prayers. They were also ready to get out of their homes and start helping one another.

One of the FEMA staff members stopped Lloyd later Sunday afternoon to announce that the agency would pull out its Emanuel POD site on Tuesday. Now that power was restored and the grocery stores were starting to reopen, the staff wanted to concentrate on other aspects of the relief effort. Faith Monroe and others expressed concern that the people in the FEMA lines wouldn't have the cash reserves to restock their homes with sufficient food and water. The FEMA staff members explained that FEMA's main role and goal in disaster work was not helping individuals but rather helping local governments repair damaged roads, bridges, sewage-treatment plants, and other vital community resources.

Jill Hanson said she'd put together donation boxes to receive food at the community worship service Wednesday night. When the sponsoring groups sent out press releases announcing the service to local radio and TV stations, they would include a request for people to bring nonperishable food items. The stores and businesses on the town square that were reopening already had collection boxes out for the same purpose. It was becoming standard operating procedure for store checkout cashiers to ask if shoppers wanted to make a contribution to one of many storm-relief funds that were starting up all over the region.

Tired but grateful, Lloyd sat with Trudy and a couple of others who had stayed behind to clean up the mess from the potluck. Most of the other members had either gone home or were already out in the community helping with the giant cleanup process. Evelyn pulled up a chair across from Lloyd and Trudy.

"Do you believe in prayer?" she asked.

"I've heard there are benefits to it. Sure. What's up?"

"This," she said holding an envelope. "These are the offerings from this morning. Not the checks and cash, though there were more of those than we expected. These are the 'how I can help' offerings. I've never been so proud of this church. You'll have to read them for yourself. Many of them wrote 'yes.' Not the majority—but quite a few. But the great part is how many said they'd host volunteers or cook meals for them or do their laundry or invite them over for a meal while they're here. It's just truly amazing. Our folks don't even know what this storm will do to their bank accounts, and here they are offering to do this. I nearly cried reading them. Here—I put some of the best ones on top. Read them for yourself. If these don't lift your spirits, we need to take your pulse to see if you're still alive."

Lloyd read them one by one and passed them around to the others sitting with him. "Clear trash." "Take pictures for insurance claims." "Take care of the stray dogs we found." "Teach my grandparents how to send out e-mails to their friends." "Cook." "Whatever. Whenever." The list went on and on.

"These should be framed," Trudy said.

"Brilliant idea," Lloyd agreed. "Let's save them until we figure out how."

They decided the council would have to decide whether to add "hosting disaster-response volunteers" to the congregation's growing list of new ministries. Lloyd said he'd do a phone survey of council members when he got home.

Lloyd was able to reach most of the council members. All of them said they wanted to support volunteers, but only three of them thought that support should include turning Emanuel's preschool center into a volunteer camp. Faith, the veteran disaster-response volunteer on council, suggested they look for a partner and co-host the camp. "Maybe we could feed them, and one of our neighbors could house them." When Lloyd passed that suggestion along, the group agreed that it seemed the best solution.

He felt relieved to have a viable suggestion to offer Lillian Yeager when he called her back. He knew just where to start. But before he called Suzanne Walker, he looked at his watch. Nine o'clock already. "Tomorrow and tomorrow," he thought as he decided it was time to end this week officially. He and Trudy sat together quietly enjoying the sound of peace and quiet in their home—aware of their good fortune and in agreement that they had just received a new kind of call.

"For now, it's enough to be where we are, to be together, and to have our boys safely tucked into their own beds. Trudy, I don't know what we're getting ourselves into, but we have to stay the course and help this community get through this somehow."

"As I recall from your installation service, the commitment was to serve God and love God's people. I think that's what you've gotten yourself into. Looks like we won't run out of things to do for a long time."

"I think you're right about that." And on that note they called it a day.

A Decision to Make

Given the many new community needs, should Emanuel postpone its pre-disaster long-range plans? After hearing the many disaster-related stories Sunday it was clear to Lloyd and the other Emanuel leaders that they wouldn't return to "normal" for a long time. The Emanuel DPR team members began to wonder if they should postpone plans to remodel and expand their facilities. Three questions arose:

1. Would there be sufficient energy to carry out these plans now?
2. Would the congregation have the finances to complete the project when so many people had to direct their personal finances to some form of recovery?

3. Should Emanuel members instead focus instead on the needs of those all around them?

The social-service arm of the denomination had already sent out one plea for funding to add staff to oversee disaster-response ministry. Finances were going to be tight, even as community needs were greater than at any time in Lloyd's twelve-year ministry in Caldwell. Did these factors indicate that they should postpone the remodeling phase of their long-range plans?

Yes. The new circumstances called for new priorities.

- Although the plan to remodel and expand the facilities was enthusiastically supported at the last congregational meeting, the situation had totally changed with the disaster. Emanuel's members were generous and would probably prefer to support their community through this disaster recovery phase.
- The energy available to upgrade their facilities would likely be considerably less now, and members would worry about honoring their capital campaign pledges.
- Ultimately, putting their own congregational plans on hold to help the community's recovery process would strengthen their mission and ministry.

No. The congregation had deferred maintenance and necessary improvements long enough.

- While members certainly wanted to be part of the recovery process, there were too many deferred-maintenance issues to postpone the Emanuel remodeling plans.
- The congregation members had actually pledged more than the capital campaign goal. Not to honor their commitments

now would be to dishonor their support and undermine ever getting adequate support for future projects.

- Upgrading Emanuel's facilities would ultimately provide the Caldwell community access to better facilities to meet future needs. If the facilities had already been remodeled, they would have been better prepared to host disaster- recovery volunteers.

Maybe. The members probably needed more time to reconsider the decision.

- Emanuel should take time to educate members, who should then decide at a congregational meeting to allow as many members as possible to help make the decision.
- No one knew how long the community would be engaged in recovery issues. The decision could be postponed a few more weeks but no longer, because construction costs would most likely rise significantly.
- The congregation should see how the finances stood after the first few months after the disaster and then decide. It was too early to know how the disaster would affect the church's financial situation.

What You Need to Know about . . .

GOVERNMENT AND NONGOVERNMENTAL AGENCY ROLES

Many people become angry and even hostile when they don't get the level of financial assistance they anticipated from agencies after a disaster. While the vast majority of both paid and volunteer staff do the best they can with the available resources, there will always be people who didn't get enough help. This situation is frustrating for everyone—the disaster victims who need the help; the staff who have to say no when they'd prefer to say yes; and the local governmental and civil servants who bear the brunt of people's frustrations. Appendix I explains how the size of the service organization affects the way it functions.

The Government's Role

- Governments at the local, state, and federal levels are all required to have disaster-response plans and capabilities. Under the larger umbrella of the Department of Homeland Security, FEMA continues to serve as the primary national responder to a disaster.
- In recent years FEMA has changed from relying on funds and resources that come directly from the federal government to relying more on contracts with corporations. For example, contracts go to various businesses to supply food or housing units to move into a disaster area. This means the people delivering the bottled water may be entering a disaster zone for the first time. It also means that should another vendor who can undersell the current supplier become available, FEMA may change vendors in mid-response.
- The typical sequence of events in a disaster is for local government officials (mayors or county judges in most cases) to call upon the state for assistance. Each state has a mandate to have a disaster plan in place.
- When a disaster's impact surpasses the state's ability to respond, the governor calls on the federal government to declare the area a federal disaster. It remains the responsibility of the state and local disaster officials to oversee the use of these resources.
- FEMA's primary concern is not individual relief, though FEMA is engaged in providing emergency supplies via its point-of-distribution system (POD) and funding for those who qualify through various grants such as Small Business

Administration low-interest loans. Additionally, FEMA focuses on helping local governments restore the community's infrastructure, such as roads, bridges, fire stations, water-management plants, electric power stations, and the like.

- Governmental entities respond to governmental needs. FEMA helps the state or local government rebuild public structures and provides help to individual families to rebuild their homes and businesses. Unfortunately, the resources are often inadequate to cover the many needs.
- The disaster is local. The resources to respond are local, state, and national—with the states often serving as the conduit between national resources and local needs.

Government-Appointed Organizations

- Organizations that assist with disaster response but are not part of a local, state, or federal government are called NGOs (nongovernmental organizations).
- Probably the best-known NGO is the American Red Cross, which has been chartered by Congress to provide specific goods and services in times of disaster—food, shelter, medical attention, and spiritual and emotional care. The Red Cross provides training for volunteers who assist in the delivery of any of these resources.

Other NGOs Engaged in Disaster Recovery Work

Members of NVOAD (National Voluntary Organizations Active in Disaster, previously noted in chapter 6) provide the majority of other services and resources in disaster relief and response. These fall generally into two categories:

- Faith-based organizations: nearly every religious group that has a national expression also has a disaster-response entity. Most of these entities are members of NVOAD.

- Some nonprofit organizations, such as United Way, exist to meet specific mission objectives but are not organized as faith-based organizations. These might include groups that exist to get humanitarian aid into disaster areas, do wildlife rescue, try to mitigate or repair environmental damage from a disaster, and the like.
- Other NGOs operate outside the NVOAD structure; they spring up in response to specific needs in a community after a disaster. Some of these are structured as nonprofit organizations, while others organize as small businesses to address disaster-related situations. While the mission and performance of such groups may be necessary and legitimate, it behooves volunteers to do their homework and learn about the organization before supporting it with their time or financial contributions.

Unaffiliated Volunteers

- Some people are just naturally drawn to the drama of a disaster and show up on their own. If you are such a person, it is strongly recommended that you try to affiliate with one of the established organizations doing disaster-recovery ministry. Your local city hall or United Way or chamber of commerce should be able to direct you to the best place to get started.

Timetable for Disaster Response

As if disasters didn't cause enough confusion, there is no standard way of describing the phases of a disaster. However, a fairly common understanding of the phases is this:

- preparation for a predictable disaster (such as a storm-related incident);
- the event itself;

- rescue and recovery operations to save lives and to search for victims;
- relief efforts to provide the minimal basics of food, water, and shelter;
- recovery work to restore individuals and communities to a state of self-sufficiency.

After the rescue and relief phase of a disaster begins to wind down, the final and longest phase starts up. This is the long-term recovery phase. Each phase of disaster recovery lasts—in very general terms—about ten times as long as the previous phase. So if it takes four days to complete the search-and-rescue operations, the relief efforts will last forty days. It will then take four hundred days—thirteen months—for the recovery phase to be more or less completed.

Many factors can cause a full recovery to take much, much longer. It may take years for a community to recover from a flood, tornado, or hurricane. A community may need decades to recover from a large-scale event such as the Oklahoma City bombing or 9/11. A community that has experienced such a major trauma never really gets over it or returns to normal—but like individuals who grieve a major loss, communities do find ways to function and move forward into a different kind of normal.

Implications for Your Congregation

Each congregation is unique and will find its own most appropriate ways to prepare for and respond to a disaster. Few congregations think much about the possibility of disaster until one happens in their community. However, it really is true that an ounce of prevention is worth a pound of cure when it comes to planning how your congregation can reduce potential losses stemming from a disaster. What might be some of the most effective ways for your congregation to prepare for and respond to a disaster?

- Disasters generally require a congregation to change plans and mission goals. For example, disasters sometimes result in new population groups moving into a community. Might this be a new outreach focus? Sometimes responding to a disaster actually rejuvenates a congregation—giving it a new purpose.
- Who among the members of your congregation have specific skills needed to help people recover from the disaster? How can your congregation most effectively identify these people and introduce them to the organizations that need their skills. See appendix G for a list of talents helpful in a disaster response ministry.
- How might a disaster-response ministry affect your congregation's current outreach programs? What current groups in your congregation might be able to help with disaster response? For example, do you have a book club that might work to replace destroyed books in a school or public library? Older youth may want to train and serve as volunteers in a disaster area. A quilting group might make quilts to send to a disaster area. Sunday-school classes could collect hygiene items to put in care packages.

Resource

Federal Emergency Management Agency, *www.fema.gov.*

Questions for Reflection

1. We all volunteer for different reasons. Think about the last time you volunteered for some project. What motivated you to say yes?
2. Sooner or later we all need a little help from our family or friends or even total strangers. Think of a time when you needed to ask for help. Where did you go? Why did you decide to go there? What response did you get?

3. Asking for or accepting help is difficult for many people. How do you feel about asking for the help you need? What makes it difficult for you to ask for or accept help?
4. Sometimes our best efforts to help someone else are met with resistance or even resentment. Have there been times when this has happened to you? If so, how did you handle it?
5. What questions or concerns do you think members of your congregation would have about hosting volunteers from out of town? How could you address these?
6. What questions or concerns do you think members of your congregation would have about taking a group of volunteers into a disaster area? How could you address these?

Scripture Reflection

Therefore, since we are surrounded by such a great cloud of witnesses, let us throw off everything that hinders and the sin that so easily entangles, and let us run with perseverance the race marked out for us.

—Hebrews 12:1

CHAPTER 8

The Community that Weeps Together

LONG-TERM RECOVERY FROM A DISASTER

The body is a unit, though it is made up of many parts;
and though all its parts are many, they form one body.
—1 Corinthians 12:12

Timeline

It is now one month since the storm. The congregation scheduled a meeting to decide whether it should go forward with its long-range plans to remodel facilities, or postpone those plans to free up funds for disaster response. Three staff people from the denomination's national disaster-response organization are now using Emanuel's facilities for office space. Hundreds of Green County residents continue to migrate from one temporary housing location to another.

Situation

On the arrival of the one-month anniversary of the storms that turned the small, laid-back city of Caldwell and surrounding Green County into a federal disaster area, people still saw evidence of the disaster everywhere they looked. Blue tarps covered nearly a quarter of the homes in the area. Vacant lots were seen where homes had stood a month before. The piles of debris were diminishing, but they were still part of the landscape. Trees and other landscaping that had stayed upright through the high winds were now slowly dying after soaking in polluted floodwaters for days. The local media managed to come up with some new angle on the storm story every day.

People whose homes and livelihoods were merely inconvenienced by the events were tired of hearing about it. They were eager to move on with their lives. Their biggest complaints were about the piles of trash that hadn't been hauled away and the traffic jams resulting from so many out-of-town people coming to respond to the storm damage. Thousands of other citizens were spending hours each week dealing with FEMA, insurance adjusters, contractors, financial institutions, and other entities about who would take responsibility for repairs and financial assistance.

Many churches in town were hosting guest staff from an assortment of nonprofit agencies that would be staying in the area for a long time. Some staff people were overseeing the volunteers, who typically arrived every Sunday afternoon to spend a week cleaning out flooded houses and other buildings. Some worked the phones and the Internet in search of more volunteers willing to come into the area to help. Some were there doing case management—which, in disaster-recovery work, aims to help people design a personal recovery plan and find the tools they need to carry it out. Flyers and other announcements about how to find a case manager were now as much a part of daily life in Green County as weather reports and high-school football scores.

Caldwell and surrounding Green County were evolving into a new class system—those who could more or less put the storm behind them and return to their typical fall activities, and those who could not.

This two-tier response to the storm and its impact on daily life even affected the timing of the Emanuel congregational meeting. The planners—Lloyd, the DPR team, and the church council members—thought that a 2:00 P.M. starting time would give members a chance to go home between worship and the meeting—time to eat, relax, and have a break before returning to church. The youth ministry team had put together games and other activities to occupy the children while the adults discussed their future. However, those with home repairs pending needed daylight hours to work; those not doing repairs wanted a break after morning worship.

The meeting's only agenda item was to decide whether to go forward with the Emanuel "Building the Future" remodeling and expansion plan, or to divert the time, energy, and finances from that project into community disaster-recovery efforts.

The congregation's long-range planning team had put together a format designed to help people remain calm during the meeting. The stress level in the community was high, and many people seemed to feel anxious. The team's goal was to create an environment of calm and quiet trust in God to direct the congregation's future. The meeting opened as usual with prayers but also allowed time for silent prayer and reflection. A congregational leader read verses from the Bible, and a full minute of silence for reflection followed. Then reflective thoughts were offered by another member. The speakers were carefully chosen to reflect different points of view—some who believed strongly that the congregation should move forward with its current long-range plans and others who were equally strong in their conviction that members needed to postpone their own plans to help their many neighbors. Before the votes were cast, Lloyd reminded everyone that the well-being of Emanuel didn't depend on which way the vote went, but rather on everyone's ability to honor the consensus of the group and to support whichever decision members made collectively.

Discussions that morning before the meeting had been intense and heated. However, as the read/reflect/pray/listen cycle got underway, people began to calm down. Gradually they began to put their personal opinions and agendas aside to focus on what would be best for both Emanuel and the community.

When a handful of people disappeared to count the votes, the choir director led the waiting congregation through an impromptu hymnfest of some old favorites. Before the vote was announced,

John Sullivan introduced the regional judicatory leader, Clarence Goodyear, who was connected to the group by videoconference. He was at his office in Yorkshire and wanted to speak a word of support for the ongoing recovery efforts and thanks for the congregation's willingness to be open to God's spirit leading it in a new direction.

The decision was close, but by a slight majority members voted to postpone their own building project in favor of focusing on rebuilding their community. Via the videoconference connection Goodyear thanked them for their passion and vision and promised to work with them in the future to accomplish the goals they were postponing. "I am confident that you will be blessed as much by this decision as your neighbors will be blessed by you. When we reach out to help another, the help always comes back around to us as well."

The need for help was visible all over Green County. Dozens of homes had been mucked out, thanks to the volunteers, but hundreds more still needed to be done. The decision not to house volunteers at Emanuel had forged a much closer friendship between Emanuel's members and those of the two neighboring congregations that were housing them. Several Emanuel members had worked as volunteers when the Red Cross shelter was open at the church. Now they teamed up to provide a hot dinner for the out-of-town volunteers five nights a week. Other members started a laundry brigade to wash mounds of volunteer-camp linens every week.

The three churches, working in cooperation with their respective national disaster-response organizations, were quickly developing a fairly well-organized system. Volunteers arrived Sunday evening for a dinner at Emanuel—provided by volunteers from several area faith groups and funded by a variety of sources. The ingredients for the dinners or the money to purchase them just seemed to arrive when they were needed. One of the partner congregations had a recently retired school dietician who planned the menus a week at time. The local news media started publishing the menus. Many residents got into the habit of buying food for the volunteers when they shopped for their own families.

The volunteers also helped defray the cost of meals by the modest twenty dollars per night they paid for the privilege of sleeping on air mattresses in large rooms, sharing limited shower facilities, working harder all day than most of them had ever worked before, and hearing heartbreaking stories everywhere they went.

The recovery phase was turning out to be a massive undertaking. Most of the local clergy now spent more time in meetings than out of them. Some of these meetings were face to face, others by conference call—in addition to the dozens of e-mails going back and forth every day. A series of networks had formed over the past month. Local congregations still had their pre-disaster ministries to oversee, and all were also engaged now in some type of disaster ministry. Coordinating all this work required many meetings.

Most Green County religious leaders put in long hours comforting and assisting those still suffering from the storm, and calls requesting appointments with clergy were more frequent than ever. The leaders also met regularly with local community governmental and social-service agencies, as well as with the newly arrived governmental and nonprofit agencies. For some, attending meetings threatened to become a full-time endeavor. People agreed that trying to keep everyone current on the recovery and soliciting input to plan the next steps was important, but keeping up was a significant challenge.

Residents who had the most resources before the storm were recovering most quickly. Some families had money set aside for an emergency, and the disaster certainly was that. Or they had friends and family who came to the rescue, or they had adequate insurance to cover most of their recovery costs.

However, the whole community was affected in some way, resulting in a ripple effect that eventually involved everyone. For example, one of Emanuel's more generous families owned a plant nursery and a large home overlooking the Green River that was flooded not once, but twice. The nursery was badly damaged, and as a result the family lost nearly all its fall business. Their home was also badly damaged by high winds that brought a tree crashing down on the roof. Although they had both business and residential property insurance, the deductibles and loss of revenue still set them back financially. They knew eventually they'd recover and be all right. However, in the short term, the financial losses meant they couldn't make their usual five-figure year-end gift to Emanuel and other causes they typically supported. The local emergency-relief agency supported by Emanuel and other congregations in town, as well as by generous individual donors, was struggling to meet the increased requests for services with reduced resources of food and clothing to disburse.

Others were now in truly desperate situations. Elderly citizens, hourly workers who hadn't been able to work for several days or more because of the storm, and single mothers who were barely making ends meet before the storm were having an especially hard time. Teachers knew that some of their students were living in the family car. Store clerks ached, watching people carefully count out their small change to see if they had enough coins to cover the milk and cereal they were buying. Doctors feared that patients weren't filling their prescriptions, or were taking only half the recommended dose. The Emanuel staff and council members were also feeling the pinch. Offerings were down by at least a third of what they normally brought in at this time of year. The repair bill for the water and wind damage to the sanctuary far exceeded what had been anticipated. The insurance adjuster reminded them that they had a 5 percent deductible on their policy, and the damage was greater than originally estimated as well. The beautiful hardwood floor had warped and would have to be replaced. The pounding rains had saturated parts of the sub-roof, and a large section would have to be reroofed.

The Red Cross shelter at Emanuel had closed six days after the storm. Volunteers and staff had worked tenaciously preparing residents to move into transitional housing. Some workers now commuted an hour each way every day between new temporary homes in Yorkshire and their regular jobs in Caldwell. Some were coming to terms with the fact that they would have to move out of the area—at least for the time being. Their homes or their workplaces or both were too damaged to function anytime soon. Those who had the option to do so moved in with relatives in other communities and looked for new jobs there. Some Caldwell residents still had homes but were commuting many miles and hours each week to jobs fifty or more miles away. The additional cost for fuel was yet another stressor.

Nearly as many vehicles with out-of-state license plates were seen around town as cars with local plates. Insurance adjusters were still in the area processing claims. Some people were pleased at how quickly the companies responded—handing them their checks the same day they inspected the damage. Others were just learning how complex and disappointing it could be to deal with the financial realities of a disaster.

Anger and frustration were the norm. The local paper was filled with letters to the editor and articles about the runarounds some people seemed to encounter at every turn. Horror stories were plentiful about the red tape residents had to deal with, adding to their stress and despair. *The Yorkshire Evening News* reported that one Caldwell man was assessed a nearly one-thousand-dollar fine for failing to return a piece of rental equipment destroyed when his home flooded.

In another part of town, one apartment complex manager had been collecting rent for several months without paying the complex's utility bills. When he realized the extent of storm damage, he packed up and left town with no intention of paying the overdue bills that continued to pile up, or of making the necessary repairs.

Now residents had been given two days' notice to vacate, because the bank was about to foreclose on the property, and both water and power would be cut off. More than five hundred already beaten-down people were going to be added to the homeless count. At the last minute the Caldwell mayor and city council stepped in to negotiate a deal with the utility companies and the out-of-state bank holding the mortgage. The county's district attorney started a search for the runaway manager, and the people were allowed to stay. Meanwhile, local government officials went in search of a new manager to coordinate repairs to the damaged units and to hold the out-of-state owner of the property accountable for the cost of repairs.

FEMA had set up shop in several locations throughout the county. Some Green County residents qualified for FEMA trailers, but a month after the storm, the trailers hadn't yet arrived. Others were waiting for news about the status of their claims and more than a little agitated about what would happen to them when the last Red Cross shelter at the fairgrounds closed after one more week. Staff of several agencies worked feverishly to locate vacant apartments while area congregations offered up classrooms or fellowship halls as emergency housing. People who had empty guest rooms were torn between offering them to total strangers and potentially putting themselves at risk, or feeling guilty about letting usable space go unused.

A town-hall meeting with the mayor, county judge, and Red Cross and FEMA staff was packed with angry, scared, frustrated, and bewildered people who were still in shock at all the changes in their lives. The officials who were trying to manage the situation were almost as frustrated as the residents.

Families that had RV trailers or campers were resigned to living in them for the time being. As the overnight temperatures started to drop, the challenges of trailer living started to rise. Storing adequate warm clothing was but one of many issues families dealt with on top of life's other ongoing post-storm hassles. The almost total lack of privacy was a hardship for those of all ages who were used to a house in which to roam. But there wasn't an open apartment in all of Green County, or even as far away as Yorkshire. Families who at least had access to campers tried to be grateful for having a roof over their heads.

Emanuel members pitched in to help support other churches that were housing volunteers from far and wide. These volunteers brought with them not only their hard work but also hope and encouragement. "Hero" stories were told and retold all over town. For example, one couple from Wisconsin closed down their catering business for three months to come cook for the volunteer camp. They graciously augmented what the Caldwell volunteers were already doing—much to the relief and delight of the local people who were wondering how long they'd have to cook for the volunteers. The couple arrived the first of October and said they'd stay through the end of the year. "And don't worry about food too much. We have connections. We'll get your folks fed." They did indeed. Between their connections back home and what the various community members were already doing, feeding the volunteers was one of the easiest parts of the recovery effort.

The problem of showers was solved when the congregations housing the volunteers got a call from their national disaster-response organization. They needed a place to park a shower trailer fitted out to provide two men's and two women's showers. It was delivered by a driver who was also a plumber and who knew how to get it hooked up.

Not to be outdone, another area congregation made connections to bring in a portable self-service laundry. It came equipped with three washing machines, three dryers, a long worktable to fold laundry, and cabinets to store clean laundry. The laundry brigade volunteers eagerly took turns keeping the little unit busy.

Yet another congregation in town offered to supply movies and games for volunteers to unwind after their hard workdays. The entire community was gratified to witness this army of goodwill moving through town.

Still, there were problems. Some volunteer groups seemed intent on determining what the folks of Caldwell needed without bothering to ask. Some showed up without checking to see if there was a need for their help and then were frustrated and nasty when the volunteer camp managers told them there were no beds available for them. One particularly independent and underprepared servant-trip leader called his denomination's national disaster-response coordinator to ask for a credit card number to put his group up at a motel in Yorkshire.

Even more troubling were the groups that wanted to use the disaster as a way to make their own youth more appreciative of the benefits they had back home. They thought exposure to the difficulties experienced by Caldwell-area youth would make their own youth more grateful. One disaster-response employee whose job was supervising volunteer work crews told Lloyd a story to demonstrate how wrong things can go when volunteers arrive unprepared and insensitive to the local situation.

The supervisor was told that a group was bringing about twenty-five people, the youngest ones age sixteen. The group showed up, however, with nearly fifty people—many of them middle-school youth. The supervisor told Lloyd, "The kids refused to listen to the safety orientation, and the adults already thought they knew it all. They didn't wear appropriate shoes or clothes for the worksite. But the worst part was that a couple of the kids got bored and started picking fights with each other. They got in the way of the ones who did want to work. Two kids got into a paint fight while I was getting more supplies for them. Their sponsors let them get away with it. 'Kids will be kids,' they said. Right. And kids don't need to be in the middle of a disaster zone, I say. It's bad enough that our own kids have to live like this. We don't need tourists here; we need help."

Clarence Goodyear just shook his head when Lloyd passed on the story. "It's a real struggle. The disaster survivors are our main concern, but to continue helping them, we need the goodwill of the volunteers who come down and then go home to report on what they've seen. I guess they just don't understand the trouble they unintentionally cause."

Clarence's life now included almost-daily conference calls with various national disaster-response personnel. The purpose of the calls was partly to coach him and other faith leaders on what to expect and how to respond to the unfolding disaster-recovery process. Disaster-response staff had warned Clarence and the others that they might run into such situations.

"Indeed," agreed Clarence. "It's enough that people suffer from the disaster. But now to have to clean up after unsupervised kids—well, it's just all very frustrating."

Three staff from Emanuel's national disaster-response organization shared office space at the church: a case manager, a volunteer coordinator, and an administrative assistant who coordinated the details related to the long-term recovery effort. This arrangement meant that regional coordinator Lillian Yeager was a regular visitor to the church. She made it a point to visit with Lloyd whenever they were both in the building at the same time. Over lunch during one visit, they got into a long conversation about the whole long-term recovery process.

"This whole recovery thing is like traveling around in a country I barely knew existed," said Lloyd.

"It is rather amazing, isn't it?"

"Unbelievable. The lengths to which people go to help. So many volunteers from so many places. People who probably vacation in upscale resorts are sleeping on air mattresses and thanking us for letting them do it—taking their vacation time to sort through rotten, smelly, awful stuff."

"Right," said Lillian, nodding. "I wish the people who get so disgruntled with organized religion could see this view of it. These volunteers are amazing, but don't overlook all your own members who help out. Even though Emanuel couldn't provide sleeping spaces for volunteers, you're doing more than your share. You cook for them; you do their laundry. I know that many volunteers have been treated to family dinners in people's homes. The people here who are hosting the volunteers have plenty of their own problems to manage right now."

"They do," Lloyd said. "And that's one thing that confuses me. Explain this whole case-management thing to me."

"Whoa. That's a tall order. It varies from disaster to disaster."

"Depending on what?"

"Several things. Funding is always a biggie. Some disasters are more popular than others and generate more relief dollars. And people like helping in some locations better than others, too."

"That's sad," said Lloyd.

"It is. But it's human nature."

"What else?"

"The size of the disaster. How much the federal government gets involved. It's a bit complicated. No, it's a *lot* complicated. But the bottom line is—money comes into a variety of agencies from various sources. Case management in one piece of the long-term recovery puzzle. Who provides these services and how the services are funded are different in every disaster. Case managers, who are often paid professionals, work with the individual families to develop each family's recovery plan."

"What is a recovery plan?" Lloyd asked.

"Think of this as humanitarian aid," Lillian suggested. "We focus on families that don't have access to other resources. We work with them to determine what they need to be able to take care of themselves and their families again. What do they need? A new place to live? Retraining to find a new line of work? Help paying for construction costs? Replacement tools they need to earn a living? Whatever it is, we work with them to define what they need most. Then all the case managers get together and go through the resources available.

"Such as?" asked Lloyd.

"Such as—access to housing in another community, or some funds to defray part of the costs of construction materials. And a crew of volunteers to help them, so they don't also have to hire labor. It goes on and on. Sometimes it seems cumbersome and inefficient to the people who depend on this system—but it really works amazingly well."

"I'll take your word for it. How many people does this involve?"

"Thousands and thousands. Again, it depends on how much funding comes in and how many people need help recovering from the disaster."

"Wow. This really is a glimpse of what we can do when we focus on helping one another."

Yes, There Is a Structure and a System. However, . . .

Each organization and agency that engages in disaster-response ministry may take on distinct functions at various disasters.

On the one hand, the agencies repeatedly involved in disaster work have evolved into an effective network, with each organization tending to focus on a specific aspect of the work. For example, generally the United Methodists focus on case management—helping people determine their own recovery plan and rounding up what they need to carry out that plan. The American Baptist men's organization shows up almost immediately to feed people—both disaster victims and the volunteers there to serve them. The Seventh-day Adventists find places to store the tons of relief items that typically start arriving within a few days. The Lutherans have reconstruction and repair of homes down to an art. The Christian Reformed World Relief Committee sends out teams to walk the neighborhood assessing the well-being of each household.

However, each disaster requires that roles and functions be redefined to meet the circumstances. Katrina required just such redefining. The devastation caused by Hurricane Katrina touched the hearts of so many people worldwide that within weeks, sixty-six million dollars had poured into the United States from foreign countries. Some of these donations came from places where the United States has dropped bombs within the past decade, or where we send relief supplies and dollars. Some of the poorest countries sent money and offers for other relief items.

These funds—known as Katrina Aid Today (KAT)—were initially managed by the Federal Emergency Management Agency (FEMA). Given that FEMA does not typically manage donor dollars, however, it quickly assigned the management of the KAT funds to the United Methodist Committee on Relief (UMCOR), with the stipulation that UMCOR appoint other partner disaster-response organizations to help administer and distribute the funds. The United Methodists are known for doing case management well. The selected partners have reputations for handling other aspects of disaster recovery well. And they were experienced enough to adjust their typical modes of operation to incorporate case management into their recovery work, in addition to other work they were doing.

These funds, earmarked specifically to provide support to victims of Katrina, provided:

- salaries for 2,259 case managers who were trained during the program—many of them hurricane victims themselves;
- offices in 131 locations in thirty-four states where people relocated;
- direct service to 192,888 people;
- $137,706,596 worth of resources accessed for Katrina survivors.

The services included helping survivors formulate their personal recovery plans, dealing with the complex system of paperwork, helping survivors advocate for additional resources to meet unmet needs, and providing counseling on an as-needed and requested basis.

In addition to UMCOR, the network of organizations receiving KAT funds included Boat People SOS, Catholic Charities USA, Episcopal Relief and Development, Lutheran Disaster Response, National Disability Rights Network, Odyssey House of Louisiana, Salvation Army, St. Vincent de Paul, and Volunteers of America.

It is unlikely we'll see such enormous levels of international aid coming into the United States for future disasters. However, the way the Katrina Aid Today fund evolved and worked to address staggering levels of need is an example of how the disaster-response community is constantly adapting and evolving with each new disaster.

"For sure. People who just want to prepare themselves for a disaster or help out when one hits don't need to know all this. But it does help to understand that there is a system in place, and that it really works pretty well. We have a saying in disaster work: 'If you've seen one disaster—you've seen one disaster.' Each one is different. But what keeps many of us going are all the stories out there about the amazing ways people come together to bring sanity out of the suffering and loss."

"So all this experience we're all getting around here won't do us any good in the next disaster?" asked Lloyd.

Lillian shook her head. "Not true. You know so much more now than you did a month ago. And that experience won't be wasted. It's a bit like cooking. You know you need to produce a meal. How you do that and what food you use will vary from meal to meal—but the skills to get the meal pulled together are used over and over, even though each meal is different."

"That makes sense. What are the most important skills?"

"Thanks for asking that," said Lillian. "Be a servant—not a savior."

"That's it?"

"Of course, there's more. But that's the starting point.

GO TO SERVE, NOT TO SAVE

Lloyd and Lillian finished their lunch and went back to their separate—but equally important—roles; he to his pastoral duties and she to check in on her staff and to visit the sites where the volunteers were working that day.

Lloyd and his colleagues had come to depend on their weekly clergy breakfasts. These Saturday-morning gatherings had become a "must be there" priority for everyone. The group included many laypeople as well as clergy. It was a diverse group by any standard—age, length of time in the community, ethnic background, level of training, theology. But the group members were in agreement that

"God-is-out-to-get-you" judgments didn't help anyone. Sadly, they were aware of a small handful of local religious leaders who didn't attend these breakfasts and whose theories about the disaster further traumatized people. Most agreed it was inhumane to promote such guilt-ridden ideologies among people who had lost so much and were so fragile.

The Saturday group members had organized a community "Talk Spot"—a place set aside in the fellowship hall of a congregation down the block from Emanuel. Each week at breakfast they passed around a sign-up sheet for the hours each would be available just to talk with people or to supply the coffee and tea for any who came.

Before the storm one Caldwell woman had gotten trained with her cocker spaniel to make hospital and nursing home visits. She volunteered to bring the dog to visit during the Talk Stop hours. At first the disaster-recovery leaders were reluctant to let her bring Freckles. But when they saw the positive response people had to Freckles, they encouraged the woman and her dog to come as often as she could. Freckles quickly won over some of the children and older people who had lost their pets in the storm.

Volunteer spiritual and emotional caregivers never knew who might wander in looking for a little reassurance. They in turn appreciated the support given them by outside chaplains from the Red Cross and various religious disaster-response agencies. Visiting chaplains were coming on a regular basis to offer care to the community's caregivers. Some of the guest chaplains offered to lead worship services, so that pastors could take a Sunday off. They also visited with community members, offering extra opportunities to talk. Sometimes they helped coordinate recovery details or visited volunteers hard at work.

Just as fall leaves were starting to change color, so too conversations around town were gradually changing from the storm damage to creative ways people were coping with the situation and caring for one another.

Lloyd and his colleagues often commented that it was sad that it took a disaster to bring a community together, but thank God they were coming together. Worshipers at the community service the Wednesday after the storm filled all 350 seats at the Green County Hospital auditorium. There had also been perhaps fifty latecomers standing along the walls. Every faith-based organization in the area was represented. In addition to readings from a variety of sacred texts, the service had included brief comments from a dozen people. The list included Mayor Eric Gulian, a Red Cross volunteer chaplain, and representatives from a half-dozen congregations.

Many people said later that the most touching message had been delivered by an eighty-seven-year-old lifelong Caldwell resident, Clara Longstreth. She had lost her home in the flood, along with all her family photos, the quilts she'd inherited from her grandmother, and virtually everything else she owned or cared about. Yet she kept telling the congregation, "But I'm not leaving here yet. I've got more work to do, and I'm going to stay here and do it."

She was true to her word. A local motel put her up in a small efficiency unit while her out-of-state family worked out a better solution for her. Every day she went out for a daily walk—trash bag in hand. When the trash bag was full of storm debris, she left it on a curb with other mounds of trash and headed back to her room. There she spent the rest of the day calling people. Clara called some because she figured they needed an encouraging word. Others she called because she thought they needed a little prodding to help poor storm victims get resituated. No one had the gumption or heart to turn down a call from Miss Clara.

Clarence Goodyear frequently told people, "Disasters always bring out the very best and the very worst we have to give each other." *This is certainly true*, thought Lloyd as he shook his head in disbelief at some of the stories he was hearing.

One of his clergy colleagues had told him over lunch yesterday about one nonprofit group that threatened to pull out its volunteers and its portable kitchen unit because the agency's name wasn't printed in large enough letters on the tractor-trailer sign. Faith Monroe had told him about asking a couple of volunteers to leave when she was doing disaster response work in Ohio. The volunteers had insisted it was not only their right but in fact their duty to pass out their religious literature, even after Red Cross staff told them that their doing so was offensive to some of the guests.

A month after the storm, things were beginning to calm down. A Green County Long-Term Recovery Committee was forming. The first meeting was called by the Caldwell Clergy Council, following the advice of a couple of professional disaster responders. City Hall was packed with fifty-five people for the first meeting.

One topic of conversation was what to do about a community Thanksgiving event. In previous years this had been one of the highlights of the month as various congregations took turns hosting it the Sunday before Thanksgiving Day. It always drew a large turnout and included mountains of food for the post-service supper, a youth choir and orchestra, and a food drive to support the local emergency relief pantry.

The obstacles this year were many. The community hall where religious groups hosted the annual event had been among the many public buildings that flooded. It was closed for repairs and not expected to reopen for a year. The woman who had been appointed coordinator of this year's event no longer lived in the area. Her family had had three feet of water in their home. Besides that, their family-owned gift shop on the town square had sustained substantial damage when a window blew out. That family had moved out of state and hadn't been heard from since. Most of the people who usually pulled together the event were too overcome by their own struggles to do so this time. Yet the community service had been such a boost to people's spirits that the area clergy didn't want to cancel it now, even though most of them were showing signs of the stress they'd been experiencing for the past month. They felt drained. They didn't have the energy to pull this off; yet they didn't have the heart to let it go.

A Decision to Make

Should Emanuel offer to host the community Thanksgiving service and supper? Emmanuel was large enough to host them both. However, the congregation had already hosted a Red Cross shelter, reopened its preschool, and provided space for a police chaplain to meet with first responders, and they were now providing office space for disaster-response staff. While some of the members seemed to be thriving on the extra activity and interaction with out-of-town people, others were starting to complain about the disruptions. Moreover, the church still had its own sanctuary repairs to manage. Some members were expressing concern about the congregation's financial position since the storm, as well as the toll on the core volunteers who would probably end up doing most of the work. Given this situation, should they offer to host the annual community event?

Yes. The community needs the continuity.

- The community worship service one week after the storm was without question meaningful. This would be another chance to bring the community together again—to give thanks for what the residents still had and for all the help they had received.
- Hosting the Thanksgiving service and supper would demonstrate that Emanuel's ministry was not dependent on having remodeled facilities; the facilities were one tool among many to do ministry.
- After the decision not to house volunteers, many Emanuel members increased their own volunteering, so the congregation probably would have the "people resources" to host the service.
- It would help Emanuel members feel better about postponing their long-range remodeling plans if they hosted this annual event.

No. Enough is enough.

- Emanuel members had already done plenty of outreach, sacrificing, stretching, and hosting.
- Maybe there didn't need to be a community Thanksgiving service this year. Maybe canceling it would be a way to affirm the reality of what everyone had been through and to provide some rest for weary workers.
- The time, energy, and money spent on this event would be better spent helping those who had lost so much.

Maybe, if enough people volunteered to help.

- If there were enough new volunteers from other congregations to help so that Emanuel members wouldn't be unduly stressed by the event, it might be good to host it.
- If donations of food and cash were sufficient, Emanuel could host it. If it would require funds from Emanuel, congregation leaders should just say "no thanks."
- The congregation should conduct an informal poll to see how many would attend if Emanuel hosted the service.

Repairing the Fabric

A disaster affects the entire fabric of community that existed prior to the event and can cause traumatic stress among the whole community. Disaster recovery is in large part the rebuilding of community, the retying of the thousands of strands of relationships in the fabric of our being together that have been severed by the disaster.

—John A. Robinson, Jr., Presbyterian Disaster Assistance, in *Light Our Way: A Guide for Spiritual Care in Times of Disaster for Disaster Response Volunteers, First Responders, and Disaster Planners* (Arlington, Va.: National Voluntary Organizations Active in Disaster, 2006).

What You Need to Know about . . .

LONG-TERM RECOVERY

After the media move on to the next big story, the adrenaline levels of those who lived through the disaster begin to return to normal levels, and everyone living in the disaster area adjusts to a "new normal" way of life, and the final and most complex phase of disaster recovery begins. This long-term recovery phase is different for each community; this process will eventually help the community rebuild not only buildings and facilities, but also lives and a new post-disaster culture.

- The first and perhaps most important thing to know about long-term recovery is that it *will* be "long term," and planning for it usually begins as the relief and rescue phases are winding down. This point may come a month or more after the disaster.
- The positive part of community long-term recovery is that it often provides a wonderful example of what humans can accomplish together when they work toward the common goal of improving the situation for everyone.
- The downside of a community long-term recovery process is that it is likely to be complex, involving dozens of organizations that have probably never before worked together, doing tasks people have probably not had to do before, under conditions of high stress and chaos.
- The long-term recovery effort generally starts just as a community is coming to grips with exactly how devastated it is. Shortly after a disaster there is typically an initial emotional high and an attitude that "this won't get us down." By the time disaster leaders are trying to launch a long-term recovery process, this attitude has probably been replaced by a generalized

state of frustration and discouragement, if not outright depression about an apparent lack of progress.

- There is no consistent way that a long-term recovery effort develops. Sometimes the effort is initiated by faith-based disaster-response organizations or other nongovernmental organizations, at other times by local governmental entities or local congregations that see the need. While no two long-term recovery efforts will be the same, the key to effectiveness is to draw on local leadership and to rely on lessons learned in other communities that have recovered from disaster.
- Disaster recovery generally presents a major financial challenge for congregations. They will likely incur unanticipated expenses that will not be covered by any other source.
- The best starting place for financial recovery is the congregation's insurance company. The sooner a claim is filed, the sooner it can be processed. Claims are processed in the order in which they are received. In a disaster zone many, many claims will be filed.
- Those who may qualify for FEMA financial support will not receive any attention from FEMA until they have filed any insurance claims, and the claims have either been paid or denied.
- Each faith group has its own way of handling financial assistance. Find out before a disaster hits how it works in your system. Some provide aid directly to a congregation; others make appeals to raise money to help rebuild a congregation. Some expect congregations to be self-sufficient. Many hurt feelings surface when expectations differ from reality. Learn in advance.
- Even the best insurance plans probably include a hefty deductible; 5 percent is not uncommon. Congregations need a rainy-day fund as much as individual families do. Congregation members will be hard-pressed to generate repair funds for the congregation when they have to cover their own home repairs.

- Congregations have a variety of sources from which to apply for grants and financial assistance. These include other congregations, judicatories, individuals, nonprofit agencies, and perhaps even government entities. However, it will generally fall to the leaders of the congregation to make the needs known and to request financial assistance. A grant writer may well become the congregation's best friend.
- The case-management part of long-term recovery will vary greatly from disaster to disaster. However, in nearly all events designated federal disasters, there will be some way for desperate people to work with a professional case worker.
- People who want the help of a case manager can help make that experience go more smoothly if they:
    - Provide some proof of disaster-related expenses.
    - Provide complete and current contact information.
    - Spell out details about immediate needs.
    - Prioritize these needs, based on the severity of each one.
    - Go in person to meet with the case manager rather than trying to work by phone or e-mail.
- Once an individual is working with a disaster case manager, he or she can expect:
    - A follow-up assessment of what kinds of help will be available.
    - Help in developing a recovery plan, including sources to meet unmet needs and action steps within a proposed time frame.
- Disaster-response organizations will be looking for people with appropriate social-work skills to help do case-management work. Congregation members with appropriate education and experience may find new employment opportunities after a disaster. Others may qualify for training to do case-management work.

- When the local congregation cannot meet someone's needs, it is appropriate to refer that person to the national disaster-response organization affiliated with the denomination or the local VOAD chapter.

Implications for Your Congregation

In a perfect world, when one congregation or community or household is hurt by a disaster, other congregations, communities, and families would assist quickly, competently, and equally. Unfortunately, we do not live in a perfect world. Resources are not evenly distributed. Disasters tend to raise anxiety to high levels. Those with the greatest needs do not always receive the most help. Your congregation needs to assume that it will have to fend for itself.

- Disaster recovery is ultimately in the hands of the people hurt by the disaster. Others will help—but they will not be able to do the hard work of recovery for your congregation or your members.
- The most effective congregations are those that develop a disaster-preparation plan and encourage their members to have their personal disaster-preparation plans in place. (See appendix H for an outline of items to put into a congregational disaster-preparedness plan.)
- Not all congregations have equal resources. Review your resources and assets—and determine how much your congregation can realistically do in response to a disaster. All willing congregations can be part of the disaster-response effort in their community. Does your congregation have access to any of the following resources?
    - › A room that visiting disaster-response staff can use to meet with individuals for case-management interviews.

- A kitchen to feed any disaster-response staff and volunteers for one meal or more a day.
- Unused or underused space to store the supplies that will be delivered to the community.
- A nursery or preschool room not in use during the week that could be designated for community child care.
- Classroom space to use for orientation sessions before volunteers go to work at a site.
- Worship or meeting space to offer other congregations or community organizations that can no longer use their regular meeting places.
- Volunteers to help existing food banks distribute some portion of resources people will need.
- A comfortable and private space for mental-health professionals to use for grief counseling.

This list is only partial. Sometimes the simplest gestures of kindness carry huge messages of support and sympathy. People who have lost much are encouraged by a bottle of water, a warm smile, a pad of paper and crayons for their children, or a quiet place to sit and rest. Ask about the need for specific items that your members can collect and distribute: eyeglasses, hearing aids, children's toys, games, books, school supplies, or office supplies.

Resources

Community Partners, ***From Chaos to Community***, *www.communitypartners.org*. A resource about how one community rebuilt following catastrophic fires.

Church World Service, ***Community Arise: A Disaster Community Curriculum***, *www.communityarise.com*. Curriculum designed to bring major faith community domestic disaster training under one umbrella.

Questions for Reflection

1. How many outside groups now use your congregation's building for meeting space?
2. List all the groups and organizations in which you now participate. Where might these groups meet if they could no longer use their regular meeting places?
3. Does your congregation have a "rainy-day" account? Is it adequate to cover three or more months of expenses?
4. Has the insurance coverage of your congregation been reviewed within the past year or so?
5. If you lost your home and your job because of a disaster, where would you turn first for help? What kind of help would you expect to receive?

Scripture Reflection

Sing to the Lord, you saints of his;
praise his holy name.
For his anger lasts only a moment,
but his favor lasts a lifetime;
weeping may remain for a night,
but rejoicing comes in the morning.
—Psalm 30:4–5

CHAPTER 9

Suffer the Little Children

HOW TRAUMA AFFECTS THE YOUNGEST AND THE OLDEST

And he took the children in his arms,
put his hands on them and blessed them.
—Mark 10:16

Timeline

Two months after the storm. The ongoing stress is particularly difficult for the community's more vulnerable members: the children, the elderly, those who struggled with physical, mental, or financial challenges before the storm. The same is true of the caregivers and those who remain homeless or jobless, or both, because of the storm. Emanuel was able to host the Thanksgiving dinner—thanks to a team of volunteers from out of town. The rescue and relief efforts have virtually ended, and the community is now in the long-term recovery phase.

Situation

The Green County long-term recovery committee was slowly getting organized. It seemed that every meeting included new people who were just learning that there was such a committee and wanted to be part of the action.

Monica and her family moved back into their home right before Thanksgiving. Volunteers had helped them gut out their first floor down to the two-by-four wood studs four feet from the floor. Other volunteers were helping them redo the first floor. The family was now living on the second floor, going to down the first floor only for the basics of cooking and laundry.

Monica was worried about some of the children in the preschool at Emanuel. She couldn't figure out what was wrong, but her instincts told her that these children were far more aware of what was happening around them than the adults in their lives realized. When she talked to Lloyd, he suggested that she start participating in the long-term recovery meetings. "You know as much about children and what they need as anyone," he said. "And I've got to reduce the number of hours per week I spend in meetings! If you went, you could brief me on what they cover. I want to stay connected, but I've got to start switching my focus back here to Emanuel and the needs of our own members. Storm or no storm, people still expect and deserve that their small groups will function, worship will happen, and support will be available when they are dealing with problems that have nothing to do with the disaster."

Monica thought it over and agreed to go. She was pleasantly surprised how cooperative and focused everyone was at her first meeting. It was obvious that people with a lot of compassion and competence were sitting around the table. Everyone signed in, and many business cards were exchanged. She learned later that this was a regular routine at every meeting, because the participants changed from meeting to meeting. The repetition of introductions might seem tedious to the core members, but the practice expanded the network and ensured a constant source of new ideas and contacts.

After the meeting, two women approached Monica with an invitation to join them for lunch, so they could continue the conversations about how best to help the children and the elderly in town. Monica thought it was an odd combination—the kids and the seniors—until one of the women, a professional social worker from out of town, explained. Jackie Lorenski had been hired by her faith group's national disaster-response organization to provide spiritual and emotional care in the community. She had taken early retirement a couple of years ago. When she heard about the storm and the terrible toll it was taking on people in the region, she called her former employer—a social-service agency—to see if there was anything she could do to help. Her grandparents had lived in Green County all their lives. Her father was raised here. He moved away to go to college and never returned except for annual summer vacations to visit his parents. Jackie hadn't been back in years, but she had fond memories of the place. She was sad thinking about the places she had frequented in her childhood that were ruined now, and the people who were suffering now. She had in mind volunteering her counseling skills for a month or two.

Her former boss persuaded her to come out of retirement and move to Caldwell for the next year or so. She agreed, and now she was making the rounds of the community. She had met most of the pastors and had established some semi-regular office hours in three locations, so people knew when to find her in an office.

Her real passion was for the elderly. Over lunch she explained to Monica, "It may seem as though we're working with two different populations. I want to work with the elderly, and you have a passion for the kids. What they have in common is that both groups are the most vulnerable and sometimes the least able to muster the resources and help they need to recover. Would you like to partner to see how we can help both these populations get through this?"

Monica liked Jackie's ideas. That day a new program was designed—sketched on the paper napkins at the restaurant where they hashed out the details. Jackie told Monica she thought her agency could find some grant money to help launch the initiative. Monica thought she could commit some space at Emanuel. "We've hosted all sorts of people and groups over the past few months. Why not one more?" She called Lloyd on her cell phone and ran the idea past him.

"Well, we can certainly find a corner to have a few people meet once in a while if that's all you need," he said.

"I don't know where this will go, but that's what we need right now."

"Consider it done. I'll check with Evelyn to see what space works out best with the other commitments we already have."

Jackie told Monica that, in general, people were holding up as well as could be expected. She and the other mental-health professionals now stationed in the area were working overtime to design programs that would expand the number of people they could reach and the variety of ways to connect them with one another. "Given the levels of stress I've been seeing, we're not going to run out of work for a very long time. Even though a lot of people are feeling lost and disoriented, some of them won't give themselves permission to talk about the pain they feel. I'm afraid we're going to start seeing a lot of physical illness in the months to come. And even when people are open to talking to someone like me, they're worried about the cost. We operate on a sliding scale and don't charge even close to what we would in a non-disaster area. But we need to get the word out, so people don't assume they can't afford us."

"I thought your expenses were covered by your agency. I'm surprised to hear you have to charge at all."

"It's an ongoing discussion," Jackie said. "By collecting some fees, we're able to stay in an area longer. The dollars donated to a disaster dry up pretty quickly—about as soon as the next disaster hits in another area. Besides, we want to do everything we can to empower people to manage their own recovery. Think of it as being like physical therapy after a car accident. We can walk alongside, we can teach and coach and encourage—but ultimately the accident victim has to do the hard work of recovering. No one can do someone else's healing for them. Asking people to pay something for our services is part of engaging them in full partnership in their own recovery."

"That makes sense," said Monica. "Maybe it's time for us to start charging a fee for the kiddos we serve at the preschool."

"I think there is something to the theory that people value what they pay for more than they value any handout they get. The notion that 'you get what you pay for' is pretty deeply entrenched in most people's minds."

"How does that work with all these volunteers who work on people's homes at no charge?"

Jackie grinned. "Every principle has an exception. There is a cost to it. The volunteers pay to stay at the volunteer camp; the homeowners generally have to find the funds to pay for the building materials. So while the homeowners don't pay for the volunteer labor, they generally do help finance the construction materials. Sometimes we can help cover the cost of housing and feeding volunteers, but even then, they've put in plenty of sweat equity for whatever good feelings they get out of the experience."

"There's so much I don't know!" Monica exclaimed. "Volunteers pay to give up their own homes and vacation time to sleep on cots and work like dogs all day?"

"Yup. That's how we can keep the camps open as long as we do. Requiring people to pay also tends to discourage people whose motives may be less than ideal—people who want to come down for a cheap tour of a different part of the country, or who come as disaster junkies."

"What do you mean?"

"It's sad but true: some people get their thrills from other people's misery. They come into a disaster area to gawk more than out of a sense of compassion. They make up only a small percentage, but they're around. Having to pay a few bucks a night tends to discourage them."

Jackie went on to tell Monica about the program she was running at the assisted-living facility adjacent to the Green County Hospital. She was now offering scrapbooking parties not only for the residents but also for anyone over fifty-five in the community who cared to join them. Participants brought any photos or other mementos they had salvaged and put them in memory books, with the help of volunteers with a flair for artistic projects.

Each book included space to write about memories of other storms they'd survived, what happened to them in this storm, and any words of wisdom they wanted to impart to their children and grandchildren. "One of our volunteers is from your church—Faith Monroe."

Monica wasn't surprised to hear that Faith had jumped into this project with great enthusiasm. Faith had lost many of her own family mementos in one of the Ohio floods. She knew firsthand the value of giving people a concrete way not only of remembering, but also of preserving their memories for future generations. Of course, many had lost their family photos in the flood. In those cases Faith and other volunteers passed out crayons, colored pencils, and markers and suggested that people draw memory pictures. Their grandchildren particularly appreciated getting such artwork from their grandparents.

Monica started thinking about ways to coordinate some joint effort between her preschool children and the older Green County residents. Jackie continued describing the program. "We're looking for volunteers to interview our seniors about their experiences, so that they can add these to their scrapbooks. This disaster isn't the first one for most of these folks. They've got some real insights into how to get through tough times. Helping them remember other hard times they've lived through sometimes helps them muster the willpower and tenacity to get through this storm.

"We're now figuring out how to get some of the community teens involved. It seems a natural. The seniors have the life experience to weather tough times. The teenagers have the tech skills to record their stories on digital recorders, so they can be preserved in computer files."

Monica's mind was racing as she went back to the Emanuel preschool. So many new possibilities were surfacing that she felt more energized than she had in weeks.

Because of Trudy's and Monica's phone calls to round up students for the reopening of the Emanuel preschool, they had nearly a full house the first Wednesday after the storm. The numbers had continued to grow until, sadly, they had to start turning children away. Grateful parents dropped children off so that they themselves could meet with FEMA representatives, contractors, and insurance adjusters.

Now, three months later, a combination of ten paid and volunteer staff members were working with more than fifty children. That the head count varied from day to day sometimes frustrated the staff members. Monica would remind them that the school program was a response to the needs of families hurt by the storm. She frequently told people, "This is the preschool that God built." Every time they thought they'd have to close because they were out of money, she said, another check arrived from somewhere. She loved the way the blend of new and longtime students was starting to look like a miniature global village. One of the teachers had suggested doing a unit on "my favorite foods" and encouraging parents to supply recipes from the cuisines of their various cultures. They all enjoyed sampling recipes for the month of November. Then right before Thanksgiving, they presented an *Emanuel Preschool Cookbook* to families.

The Emanuel DPR team and council had struggled over the question of hosting the annual community Thanksgiving service and meal. They clearly saw the need to gather people together. With all the money and volunteers that had poured into the community over the past few months, they had much for which to be thankful. They remembered the healing energy of the one-week anniversary community service. But they also realized how weary people were becoming. Conditions were far from returning to normal. The media had moved on to other stories. The donations that had poured in initially were slowing down as new disasters drew attention. The volunteers were still coming in large numbers, and though residents were genuinely grateful for all the volunteer help, they sometimes admitted to one another that having so many outsiders around all the time reminded them of the times when they had wished houseguests would go home. People had an unspoken wish to have their town back to themselves.

Few voiced this sentiment aloud. They knew they needed the outside helpers, and they were grateful. But seeing them around town was a constant reminder of how the storm had disrupted their lives. People wanted to quit hearing about the storm, but as a topic of conversation it was inescapable.

One huge blessing that came with the out-of-town volunteers was the formation of a network with congregations all over the country. So it was that Lloyd was talking over dinner at Emanuel with a pastor in town for a week of volunteer work. When Pastor Rick Fenner asked him how things were going—a question Lloyd had already answered at least a hundred times in recent days—Lloyd sighed. Then he told Rick about Emanuel's dilemma—whether to host the Thanksgiving dinner.

The pastor listened sympathetically but didn't say much. The next day he stopped by Lloyd's office with a huge grin on his face. "If all you had to do about the Thanksgiving community event was to give directions to other people and eat turkey, would you feel better about hosting it?"

"I suppose, but you and I both know it's never that easy. Events don't organize themselves."

"No, but I have a crew of folks back home who are ready to swarm in to prepare a full Thanksgiving dinner for as many people as you tell us are coming. We'll come back early enough to do our shopping here—to support the local economy—and I'll plan and lead as much or as little of the service as you like. We're supposed to head home Saturday. I can postpone leaving until after that weekly breakfast you were telling me about, if that would help."

Lloyd didn't know how to respond. He was trying to envision whether this offer of help was practical. "I'll think about it and let you know. Will you be eating here again tonight?" They agreed to talk at dinner. Lloyd called a couple of his colleagues with the unanticipated offer. Both clergy were enthusiastic about it but agreed that the other Saturday-breakfast folks should get a chance to get in on the conversation.

Over coffee and dessert that evening, Lloyd accepted Pastor Rick Fenner's offer to come to the breakfast Saturday. By the time Saturday rolled around, Rick had phoned several more members of his California congregation. They all wanted to be part of providing a Thanksgiving service and dinner for the community. Their children's choir director offered to bring some of the children to sing. All the members on this mission trip to Caldwell wanted to come back, this time with the rest of their families. They would bring the bulletins for the service. They would bring table coverings and anything else needed to put on the feast. Their only concern was housing.

Over breakfast the group worked out a tentative plan. If volunteers would also bring their own cots and bedding, a couple of churches that weren't already hosting volunteers could host them for a long Thanksgiving weekend. In fact, they realized, this might not be necessary since churches now hosting volunteers didn't expect to have any over the Thanksgiving weekend. The long-term recovery team had been advised by the disaster-response professionals to take a break for Thanksgiving.

Some Caldwell citizens wanted to let volunteers work over the Thanksgiving weekend, because so many people had that time available. However, the residents and disaster-response staff who tended to the volunteer camps and organized the work projects needed a break. Volunteers coming for the sole purpose of providing the Thanksgiving dinner and supporting the service might be a nice compromise. It would provide a break from the weekly process of welcoming strangers and getting them settled into work projects, and yet it would also gather the community to focus on something positive—and to give thanks for the progress made so far.

Most of the pastors were undecided as to how much they wanted to participate in the service. In the end, they decided to use the order for last year's community service. The only change would be that instead of a sermon from one of them, two or three of them would share the sermon time. They all wanted to express their thanks for the way the community members were helping one another and share an encouraging word about the recovery process. Rick Fenner and the members of his congregation would be acknowledged for their above-and-beyond support to the community. The offering would go to the long-term recovery committee to disburse as its members deemed most appropriate.

As the residents of Green County watched the leaves start to fall, the days grow shorter, and the temperatures drop, a new kind of "normal" began to settle in around them. By now they had all accepted that there was no going back to the way life was before the storm. They were also slowly coming to grips with just how long the recovery process would take.

Gradually a low-grade depression was settling in among some Green County residents. Many adults were so distracted by the details of recovery that they didn't notice the changes in their children or teenagers. Children who had been fairly even-tempered and calm before the big storm in September were now anxious about things that hadn't bothered them before. One mother took her two grade-schoolers to visit relatives in Texas while waiting for the Caldwell schools to reopen. She said her children had always been nervous about storms, but this time they became nearly hysterical when they heard the thunder and saw lightning while visiting their Texas grandparents. Parents naturally worried about their children's anxieties, but many just hoped their children would adapt quickly. Some hoped their children were too young to understand what had happened or were distracted by playing with their friends. "They'll bounce back," parents and teachers predicted.

Monica observed behavior at the preschool and in her own grade-school children, though, that troubled her. Several of the preschoolers had become difficult for the teachers to manage. Some were biting and fighting more than usual. Some had become so quiet that it was difficult to get them to talk at all. Parents reported that their children were having nightmares or bedwetting. Some were "forgetting" to use the bathroom at school.

Parents with older children and teens also observed distressing behavior in their sons and daughters. Bewildered parents didn't know if they were dealing with normal hormone-driven mood changes or something more complicated. What they knew was that sometimes their young people expressed extreme anger and frustration, followed by apathy and a sense of uselessness. Many teens were reluctant to talk.

Jackie assured Monica that the reactions of these children and their parents were common. "For some of these young people, the situation is just too big—they don't know how to talk about it. It's not that they won't, or don't want to; it's more likely that they don't know how."

She told Monica about a program for children and youth she'd learned about called "Camp Comeback." It was a day camp designed for children who'd experienced a community disaster. It started in response to children who had survived floods, but it had been revamped along the way to include children who had experienced community-wide violence such as the events of 9/11, or a sniper incident.

Jackie explained that the idea was to use a variety of child-appropriate activities in a day-camp setting. Children would participate in a safe, lively environment with adults who understood their stress from the disaster and other children who'd had similar experiences. The program made use of teenagers as junior counselors—giving teens a chance to work through their own trauma without the pressure of being expected to talk about it directly. Children would have a chance to draw, play, sing, and talk about their experiences and hear stories of people who had survived trauma.

Common Child and Youth Reactions to Disaster

Adults may not realize, or may be in denial about, the emotional impact of trauma on the young. But pastors, youth directors, teachers, coaches, and other professionals who work with children and teens attest to the variety of ways trauma affects emotional development. Recent brain research has documented that the developing brain is changed as a result of trauma. Early intervention can make a difference in how a child will function years after the trauma is past.

- Children and teens are affected by stress as much as or even more than adults, but they manage stress differently. They don't have as much life experience of coming through difficult times to help them put things in perspective.
- Children and teens often want to talk about what they've been through but need help finding ways to express their experiences and feelings appropriately.

- Children commonly fear that they will be hurt or hurt again after a disaster. These fears can take a long time to get over. After flooding in one community, parents reported that children became panic-stricken the next time there was a heavy rain.
- Children may have nightmares and regress to earlier developmental phases, such as wetting themselves, using baby talk, or appearing incapable of doing tasks they had previously mastered. It's common knowledge among professionals who work with highly stressed people that "when we stress, we regress." Adults typically become less able to function as well as they did before the stress; children tend to regress to an earlier developmental level.
- As soon as possible, caregivers should re-establish predictable routines for dressing, eating, going to bed, and other activities to help give a child a sense that things are returning to familiar patterns.
- While it is important to help a child talk about what he or she has experienced, it is also important to focus on the strengths and coping skills the child has.
- One goal of working with disaster-traumatized children or teens should be to help them increase their resiliency. Another goal might be to help them incorporate the experience into their life story, so that it becomes one part of their biography and not the central focus of it.
- To help children recover from trauma, we must also provide parents the resources to help their own children. Intergenerational support is more effective than segregating individuals by age groups.
- Children and teens should be told the truth about what is happening, at a level appropriate for their age. Adults who lie or refuse to give accurate information about what happened or what will happen next increase children's fear and anxiety. For example, if the family home was destroyed beyond repair, parents should say so upfront and then talk about where the

family will live instead. Or if the parents don't know where the family will live, they can say so and assure the child or teen that home will be wherever the family is all together. Accurate, age-appropriate information—even bad or sad information—is a powerful remedy for anxiety. Let the child's or teen's questions guide the answers.

- Children or teens who continue to manifest stress symptoms should have the opportunity to meet with a professional counselor. Some of these symptoms include extreme changes in sleep or eating patterns, bursts of unprovoked anger or tears, and withdrawal and refusal to play or socialize with family and friends. Any form of abuse or addictive behavior—self-mutilation; use of drugs, alcohol, or other substances; or reckless behavior—should be addressed.
- If you think a child or young person needs help, trust your instincts and work with his or her parents to get the help.

Monica thought the camp sounded perfect for the Caldwell community, and Jackie offered to get the information for her. They discussed finding a way to serve some of the community's elderly disaster survivors and to help the youth at the same time. They decided to ask whether some of the participants in the scrapbooking project might consider being camp grandparents if Emanuel sponsored a Camp Comeback in Caldwell. Jackie agreed to discuss the idea with the people at the assisted-living facility. Monica offered to talk it over with the Emanuel DPR team.

When the two checked in again, Jackie reported that several of the assisted-living residents said they'd love the chance to help with the camp. Others said they didn't think they were up to it, but suggested that camp staff bring the kids to them to sing songs or play games together. Many of these older adults were excited about the idea of having more contact with children. "Never thought I'd admit this," said one woman in her mid-eighties, "but I kind of miss all the noise the little ones make."

Helping Seniors after a Disaster

In many ways the needs of people experiencing post-disaster stress symptoms are pretty much the same for everyone. That is, the traumatized need safe shelter, adequate food, water, clothing, and rest; and caring people to support them as they regain their equilibrium and figure out what to do next. On the other hand, specific factors such as age and overall physical and mental health can greatly influence how an individual responds to trauma and how effectively he or she begins to stabilize and recover.

- An older adult may require additional help to recover from a disaster. Needing help does not automatically mean that the older person is frail or helpless. Most older adults can make appropriate decisions regarding their own recovery plans, but may need help to carry out their plans. By the time one is old enough to be labeled "elderly," he or she has negotiated many decisions—both large and small. Depending on the nature of the disaster and what happened to the person as a result, however, an older adult may need extra time and support to take on yet another major life challenge.
- Every older person is an individual. Some will be able to apply lessons learned from previous setbacks to their current situation. For others, a disaster may be the "last straw" in a long series of losses. The accumulation of losses may result in reduced energy for coping and an attitude of "what's the use?" This reaction is particularly likely if the person has recently lost a mate or moved away from a familiar home because of diminished ability to cope.
- It is common for older adults to want to make sense of a disaster. They may do this by repeating stories about what happened to them and their loved ones. It is an act of kindness to listen patiently to the repetitions, which may help that person regain a sense of control and hope. Repeating the same stories over and over doesn't necessarily indicate senility; the behavior may indicate healing and working to put the events in perspective.

- Older adults with limited mobility will need physical help doing repairs and getting out to handle disaster-related business.
- Older adults may have already "downsized," letting go of many favorite things. Losing what few personal things they've saved can be extremely difficult to accept. Helping them record their memories is one way to help compensate for these losses.
- Older adults who are geographically or emotionally distant from their families may become so despondent that they start to wonder whether they should continue living. Thus, a disaster becomes a spiritual crisis as well as a physical one. Don't ignore or dismiss an older adult's comments about life's feeling pointless. Do what you can to provide an opportunity for the person to talk with a mental-health professional.
- Older adults may be unaware of various social-service resources available to them or be intimidated by the many forms to fill out or the need to retrieve information from websites. An offer to help handle some of the necessary paperwork would probably be most welcome.
- Older adults may be dealing with loneliness related to the death of a mate, health problems, or limited finances that make disaster-recovery work more challenging than it is for younger people.
- Offer information about where older people can get additional help, but do so in a way that leaves them in charge of soliciting the help, unless you are specifically asked to do it for them. Even though the trauma of the disaster may cause people to act as though they are incapable of making appropriate choices, the recovery is still their responsibility unless their actions might endanger their life or the life of someone else.
- Companionship is a powerful motivator for many people. Lack of regular companionship is often a factor in a lack of energy or interest to tend to the details of disaster recovery. Linking older adults with a network of people of similar age and interests may not seem like disaster-recovery work, but it may well be the best help of all.

The DPR team had asked Monica to get more information. How much would it cost? How much staff would be needed to pull this off? How many children could be served? Of what ages? Monica had agreed to find out and get back to them.

Jackie explained that volunteers were already trained and ready to go on the road to provide the camp experience in other communities. The cost depended on how much the local host congregations wanted to pay and how much they expected participating families to pay. The camp program was designed to handle as many children as the host congregation had space and volunteers to manage. The camp guidelines required one adult volunteer for every six to eight children that registered, but the camp could get by with a few less if there were teenagers to handle snacks and playground games. The camp was designed for grade-school children. There were also some games and activities appropriate for younger children in a preschool. Monica liked that option. Lloyd said he liked the idea of including the teens in the program.

At the next DPR team meeting the group members agreed that the camp sounded like a good idea. However, they still had some reservations about how much work would be involved on their part. They also wondered when to offer the program. Christmas break seemed too soon. Next summer seemed too far away. They settled on spring break. After making these preliminary decisions, they presented the idea to the church council at Emanuel and to the Green County Long-Term Recovery Committee. They wanted council support to host the camp at Emanuel, and they were hoping the Long-Term Recovery Committee might have some funds available to offset the cost—a minimum of fifteen hundred dollars to pay for the materials and the one staff person who would come with the camp to oversee it.

Two months after the storm, people were experiencing mixed emotions. On one hand, people still struggled to accept how much their daily lives had been changed by storm-related damage. On the other hand, most people were doing all they could to help one another heal and to find reasons to be hopeful about the future. Gradually, feelings of despair and grief were becoming less intense and less frequent, while feelings of confidence and optimism grew. Truly, there was much for which to be thankful, even amid unwelcome changes.

A Decision to Make

Should Emanuel host Camp Comeback over spring vacation?

Parents whose children have participated in such programs report dramatic improvements in their children. They become calmer, more confident, and less fearful. However, hosting such an event, even with generous volunteer support from other communities, requires coordination and planning. The congregation struggling to recover may find it difficult to offer anything new—even something with a proven track record.

Yes. The need is so great—how can we not do this?

- The program comes with staff to coordinate it, volunteers to work with the children, and all the program materials needed.
- We have a good group of our own volunteers who will pitch in to help.
- We do have the facilities, and the preschool rooms won't be in use during spring break.

No. Enough is enough.

- We've done our fair share, and our people don't need one more thing to think about.
- We don't have any idea how many children might actually enroll in this program. It seems too unpredictable to coordinate.

- Who's going to be liable if someone gets hurt? While both Emanuel and the Camp Comeback program carry insurance, the conversations about the program didn't make clear whose insurance would cover any injuries or damage. (Note: These issues are negotiable between the hosting congregation and the sponsoring organization offering the program. It is handled on a case-by-case basis each time a program is offered).
- Our people are ready to slow down and take a break. Spring break is the ideal time for the community to rest from all the storm-related work.

Maybe. We need more information.

- We've made some good connections with other congregations, both locally and elsewhere in our denomination. Let's see if we can partner with others to get this done.
- Maybe our judicatory can give us some grant money to hire someone to oversee the program. If funds were designated to hire a camp coordinator, they would provide some income for one person currently out of work because of the storm. Having a paid staff person on site would also make the work of volunteers easier.
- Maybe we can bring in someone from another disaster area who has been involved in the program to help us organize for it.

What You Need to Know about . . .

THE EMOTIONAL IMPACT OF TRAUMA

Anyone who has not lived through a horrifying disaster can never know what that experience was like for those who have been through the terror and panic. Therefore, it is best to enter a disaster area with respect, humility, and an attitude of willingness to learn and an eagerness to serve where needed by doing what needs to be done.

Opinions about how disaster survivors should respond are best kept to oneself.

- Emotional trauma and stress may generate behavior that seems unpredictable and peculiar to those not accustomed to working with a highly traumatized population.
- Children especially may have a difficult time understanding what has happened to them and the community around them. Children generally don't have the ability to talk about the distress they are feeling. The stress shows up in somatic complaints in various parts of the body. It is not unusual for a child to regress to an earlier stage of development after experiencing a severe stress or trauma. For example, a child who had previously mastered toilet training might seem to forget this skill. A child may also express trauma through physical symptoms. It is common to hear stressed people complaining of stomachaches or headaches. Distress might also be displayed emotionally in sullenness, anger, or unusual hyperactivity.
- People expressing these common symptoms of stress can often be helped with some basic coping mechanisms. These mechanisms include:
    - › Talking, writing, drawing, or other creative outlets.
    - › Finding ways to assert some control over the world, such as establishing predictable schedules, doing activities to prepare for future disasters, and mastering the vocabulary to describe what happened.
    - › Sharing experiences with other people who've been through similar events.
    - › Serving others who need help recovering from a loss or setback.
- Programs such as Camp Comeback help provide children with these skills and experiences. Congregations can also provide opportunities for children, families, and others in the com-

munity to work through their disaster experiences with new or existing programs. The scrapbooking project at the assisted-living center is one such example.

- These types of interventions will be sufficient in most cases. However, those working with survivors of traumatic experiences should be aware that some people may need more support and should be referred for professional help.

Implications for Your Congregation

Just as individuals have different gifts to contribute to a project or cause, so too congregations vary in their ability to respond to various aspects of disaster response. Use these questions to help assess the best use of your congregation's facilities and members in a disaster response situation.

- Is your congregation prepared to offer emotional and spiritual care, or would you be better off referring people to mental-health professionals?
- Do you have a network of agencies and professionals to turn to as you discover people who need specialized support?
- What structures are in place to provide emotional and spiritual care for your own congregational leaders, who may be coping with high levels of stress?
- If you partner with a disaster-response organization or a program for mental-health care, how will you define what each entity will provide? Both the congregation and the agency need to understand what each offers the other. For example, the congregation might offer space, staff support, or financial support. The agency might provide trained staff available to congregational staff and members, as well as other clients; training events on mental health topics; and introductions to other community resources.

Resources

Camp Noah, *www.campnoah.org*. A day-camp program for grade-school children who are experiencing trauma from disasters.

Hal Shope, ***God's Can Do Kids and Gearing Up—Renew U*** (Chicago: ELCA Disaster Response, 2006). Curricula for children and youth for congregational use after disaster.

James V. Gambone and Jennifer Norris Peterson, ***Together for Tomorrow: Building Community through Intergenerational Dialogue*** (Minneapolis: Elder Eye, 1977).

Norma Gordon, ***Children and Disasters***; Series in Trauma and Loss (New York: Routledge, 1999).

Questions for Reflection

1. Think back to your childhood. Do you remember any potentially dangerous situations you experienced? If so, what were they like for you? Who helped you during that time?
2. Do you know any older adults who can share stories about living through a war, the Great Depression, or other national events? If so, consider asking them to talk about those experiences. Recording their stories could provide a powerful living testimony to how people face adversity.
3. Have you had any experiences with summer camps or retreats? If so, what were those experiences like for you? Are there some elements of those events you could re-create in your congregation?
4. Does your congregation have mental-health professionals who could be asked to lead workshops on mental-health topics?
5. Could small groups already meeting in your congregation—for example, a choir, youth group, older-adult fellowship

group, quilting group—be transformed into safe places to offer mutual support should your area experience a disaster?

6. Do you know where to refer someone who is working with a child or older family member struggling to overcome some major trauma? If not, consider developing a referral list of professionals who could help such people, and make this information available to your congregation via postings on bulletin boards and in newsletters or as links on your website.

Scripture Reflection

No, in all these things we are more than conquerors through him who loved us. For I am convinced that neither death nor life, neither angels nor demons, neither the present nor the future, nor any powers, neither height nor depth, nor anything else in all creation, will be able to separate us from the love of God that is in Christ Jesus our Lord.

—Romans 8:37–39

CHAPTER 10

No Going Back

RESILIENCY AND DISASTER RECOVERY

See, the home of God is among mortals.
He will dwell with them;
they will be his peoples,
and God himself will be with them;
he will wipe every tear from their eyes.
Death will be no more;
mourning and crying and pain will be no more. . . .
"See, I am making all things new."
—Revelation 21:3b–5 NRSV

Timeline

February, six months after the storm and the first cycle of holidays after the disaster. The Emanuel council agreed to host a spring-break Camp Comeback program for grade-school children.

Situation

"The storm" had become the unofficial marker of time. People now referred to personal and community events as having happened before or after the storm.

The outpouring of support from strangers and other communities was amazing. In addition to the tremendous help, this show of concern did miracles for people's morale. *The Caldwell Courier* carried a letter to the editor from a town named Caldwell in another state, five hundred miles away. That other Caldwell had been severely damaged by tornadoes three years earlier. The gist of the letter was, "We got through our disaster, and you'll get through yours. We're praying for you all." It was signed by the head of that Caldwell's tourism and economic development office.

Encouragement from Afar

Kate Wilkes, executive director of Florida's Santa Rosa County Tourism and Development Committee, wrote to the *Houston Chronicle*:

> *It is with great empathy that I write this letter to the residents of the Texas Gulf Coast. Just a few years ago, our beautiful area of Florida was devastated by back-to-back hurricanes. . . . Hurricanes Ivan and Dennis left our area—like yours—looking like a war zone. . . . We urge you to support each other and the many souls who come from near and far to aid in the restoration. These include the utility workers, first responders, Red Cross, Salvation Army, numerous faith-based organizations and countless volunteers. Cheer on, too, the many community leaders who have a daunting task before them. . . . Keep the faith, have patience and never stop looking toward the future.*
>
> —Letters to the Editor
> *Houston Chronicle*
> October 20, 2008

After their students had missed nearly three weeks of school in the fall and then been out for the holiday breaks, teachers were finding it difficult to get them focused on schoolwork. The school board opted not to extend school or reduce the number of regular holidays to make up for the missed days, on the theory that the families would need those breaks to be together or to visit other friends and family members.

When the Emanuel DPR team and other involved people learned of this decision, they decided to host a Camp Comeback over spring break—which would fall the first week of March. Monica and Trudy were working closely with Jackie to plan for the event. The Camp Comeback program fee paid for the support of a staff member from the disaster-response organization that developed the concept. Dana Scofield, a former grade-school principal, was hired by the disaster-recovery organization to coordinate Camp Comeback events wherever they were offered.

Dana had been coordinating Camp Comeback events in response to various disasters ranging from hurricanes to fires to the recent flooding in Green County. Her agency worked on the premise that people in the disaster area already had more than enough to do, so her agency tried to keep requirements for community volunteers and resources to a minimum. Nonetheless, there was still plenty of work to be done—and, fortunately, plenty of people eager to pitch in to help.

Peg Mitchell, a volunteer looking for a cause after the initial need to distribute emergency supplies of food and water, agreed to round up all the necessary camp supplies, including snacks, art supplies, game and recreation equipment, and shoebox-sized plastic boxes that would be used as personalized emergency kits. Campers would spend the week talking about what sorts of things they had needed when their homes flooded. By the end of the week each would have a small stuffed animal, a child-size flashlight, a whistle, a laminated list of family phone numbers and other contact information, and other items to put in their personal emergency kits—"just in case." Jackie's focus was on rounding up men and women who wanted to be camp grandparents.

Work was still a challenge for many Caldwell area residents. Businesses that were open again were feeling the financial impact of the storm; revenue was definitely down. People were spending money only on essentials. Many workers who had been laid off were still struggling to find new jobs. Some businesses had decided not to reopen because the cost of repairs was too great. The look of the

Caldwell downtown area was heartbreaking. Families that had owned shops in town for generations had closed those businesses. Some businesses had "For Sale" signs posted. Others just sat empty while people tried to decide what to do next. Some local residents put out of work by the storm were finding new work on construction crews, or doing data entry for insurance companies and other response agencies, or helping with case management.

The Thanksgiving service and supper had proved a boost to local morale. Residents of Green County were trying to be optimistic and pleasant to one another. But all too often their faces and their tone of voice revealed how fearful and worn out people really were. The end-of-the-year holidays had been particularly difficult for some families. Those who typically traveled over the holidays stayed home to conserve money for storm repairs. Those still living in makeshift housing didn't feel up to much decorating and celebrating. Some felt distressed all over again when they realized how many of their holiday decorations and special mementos had been destroyed in the flood—another painful reminder of loss.

Amid the tragedy, there was also humor and pathos. One story circulating through town was generally interpreted to indicate that God was watching over them, albeit in some pretty strange ways. Two local boys found a silverware chest and took it home to inspect. The name plate, clearly visible, read GEORGE F. MCKNIT. The boys' father tracked down the McKnit family, who lived about twenty-five miles upriver from Caldwell. When the boys' father called the family, George McKnit said, "Can't be. That silver chest got stolen more than ten years ago!" By some strange twist of fate, what was once lost had been found because of the storm. Somehow this story gave people a bit of hope that God really does bring good out of loss and suffering.

Many people felt as though they were balancing on a see-saw. One day they felt optimistic and hopeful. The next day they felt overwhelmed and doubtful. Sometimes these ups and downs changed in a matter of hours. Emotional triggers were everywhere. Little slices of life constantly reminded people that their pre-storm lives were gone and that there was no going back. It was time to start over.

Lloyd Albright and his family were not immune to this phenomenon. The national disaster-response organization staff had coached Clarence Goodyear that his clergy staff would start running out of steam sooner or later. It was starting to happen for Lloyd now, six months after the disaster. Clarence offered to send in a recently retired pastor to serve as a long-term supply pastor to help out. He knew that Lloyd was putting in too many sixteen-hour days and wouldn't be able to keep up the pace. Something had to give. It might be Lloyd's health, his marriage, his effectiveness—Clarence didn't know what—but he worried that negative consequences would result from the strain Lloyd and other church leaders had been under for the past six months.

Lloyd respectfully declined the offer for help, telling Clarence, "My people need me right now. A stranger wouldn't understand what they've been through." Both Trudy and Evelyn had urged him to reconsider. Evelyn was even more aware than Trudy of how short-tempered and absentminded Lloyd had become recently. By the time Trudy saw him most nights, he was talked out and withdrawn. Their evening routine was typically to agree not to talk about the storm at all. But since the storm was still dominating nearly every aspect of community life, they usually ended up swapping storm stories before dropping into bed exhausted.

Trudy worried about Lloyd but figured he'd work things out in his own time in his own way. However, at the office, Evelyn was frequently catching Lloyd in memory lapses. She knew Lloyd had missed more than one appointment because he forgot to check his calendar. Some of the congregational leaders asked her about his health after he insisted he knew nothing about decisions made at a meeting he had attended. More and more, he had been refusing to take phone calls or return them.

It was a child who led Lloyd to the conclusion that he needed help and that his whole family needed some time to themselves.

When eight-year-old Jared asked his dad why they never played together anymore, Lloyd got the message. He was caught short by his son's plea for more of his time. Storm or no storm, Lloyd didn't want to lose his son's respect.

The next morning he made an appointment with Clarence Goodyear. The outcome was the decision that the Albright family would take a spring-break vacation. At first Lloyd balked at the idea, insisting he had to be around for Camp Comeback. Trudy admitted she'd like to be part of it too. But Clarence said he would send in a retired pastor with volunteer experience in another disaster area's Camp Comeback. Clarence suggested that the Albright family could do more good by getting away from Caldwell for a few days than by immersing themselves in yet more stories of loss and suffering.

Both Lloyd and Trudy admitted that they were looking forward to some time away. They were especially excited after Jill Hanson's surprise visit to Lloyd's office after church one Sunday. She handed him an envelope filled with twenty-, fifty-, and even a couple of hundred-dollar bills. "What's this?" Lloyd asked.

"It's the Albright family vacation fund." She explained that though many people were struggling themselves, they wanted to make sure the Albrights were still with them by the one-year anniversary of the flood. "We took up a little collection. This is from some of our members and a fair number of the volunteers we've been feeding around here." Lloyd was too touched to say anything. The tears in his eyes said it all. Jill gave him a quick hug and slipped out of the office.

Lloyd tried to pray but couldn't find the words to do that either. Evelyn stopped by to pick up her purse before going home and found him standing there holding the envelope and silently weeping.

Lloyd managed to ask, "Did you know about this?"

She nodded. "The Lord provides." She too gave him a hug and left him alone to wonder at the amazing ways God sends hope. It would be good to go to a vacation spot where the storm wasn't virtually the only topic of conversation. The Albrights spent the rest of the afternoon tossing out ideas about where to go for their trip.

Lloyd was amazed at how much more energy he had, now that he'd decided he could give himself and his family the gift of time away from the despair, depression, frustration, and crushing workload. Like nearly everyone around him, Lloyd had kept pushing so hard on recovery work that he was out of touch with his own state of mental and physical health.

As a school administrator, Trudy was also seeing symptoms of stress in teachers and students. She was glad that the Emanuel council saw the wisdom of offering the Camp Comeback program to the community. In her opinion, spring break and the day-camp program couldn't get here fast enough.

Mental-health issues at the community level were becoming an issue for all sorts of people. The initial "We shall rise again" attitude was gradually slipping into a more subdued "What's the use?" All over town, tempers were short, memories were lapsing, and energy to handle the day-to-day details of life was waning. For example, at the Green County Hospital, Hal Beckman recognized these and other post-traumatic reactions from his experiences in New Orleans after Hurricane Katrina. He was more aware than many others how important it was to provide more professional counselors to provide spiritual and emotional care for these people. However, Hal's efforts to get hospital staff to bring in these professionals were not proving very successful. But Hal was determined. He believed that the future health of some community leaders depended on having access to such professional help. So he started making phone calls on his own. He called people he knew from his Louisiana days in search of mental-health professionals willing to come to Green County to provide emotional and spiritual care for hurting people.

Eventually Hal's determination began to pay off. A few of his hospital colleagues suggested a conference call linking some of the community leaders with mental-health professionals who were still working in other disaster areas, years after the initial traumatic event. The purpose of the conference call was to review what these community leaders should expect in the coming months by way of people's emotional recovery. Relieved that the situation was being taken seriously, Hal reverted to his more familiar role as telecommunications professional charged with setting up the conference calls.

Meanwhile, Lloyd soon learned that the long-term supply pastor Clarence Goodyear planned to send in was not a newly retired pastor after all, but a highly active one—the Rev. Rick Fenner, the pastor who had spearheaded the amazing volunteer effort that made possible the annual Caldwell community Thanksgiving event.

When Clarence announced the news, Lloyd asked how he had managed to snag Rick for a supply-pastor stint. "He has his own congregation. It's amazing what they've already done for us. But how can he leave his parish to come back here for three months?"

"It seems you've gotten under his skin, so to speak," Clarence said. "Between the volunteers who have been down here and the success of the Thanksgiving service and supper, they just can't seem to do enough for you. You've all made quite an impression on them."

"But who's going to take care of *his* congregation?"

"Well, it seems a newly retired pastor moved to his town and was asking if there was anything she could do to help out. Pastor Fenner asked her if she'd like to come out of retirement for three months to free him up to come here." Lloyd was stunned.

Meanwhile Monica and Jackie continued their cross-generational recovery plans. Rather than wait for Camp Comeback, they started inviting some of the older people Jackie had worked with to spend time with the younger children. Some came to the preschool a couple of times a week to read stories or work puzzles with the children. Once a month some parents took their children to the assisted-living center for similar activities. The staff at the center made sure fresh cookies and milk were on hand. The staff also passed around paper and crayons for intergenerational drawing sessions. The benefits to all involved were visible in the smiles and hugs exchanged. The piano in the community room was in use again too, as children and surrogate grandparents plunked out some of their favorite songs. The mutual benefits were too great to number. Everyone looked forward to the days the children came to visit. Likewise, at the preschool the children got excited whenever their teachers announced it was "Grandparents' Day."

This "we're moving on" attitude seemed to be contagious. Although the number of volunteers was dropping, plenty of them stayed around to make a positive difference. They not only worked hard: they spent money on local merchandise to take home. One creative group came to town with plastic storage containers full of bulbs and seeds. They asked for leads on places to plant them and spent several hours doing yard work, along with tackling other recovery tasks.

Monica and Trudy put together a small team of Camp Comeback recruiters. The team made posters, paid to have a banner made to hang downtown, and visited every classroom it could find in the county. Team members wanted to enroll as many children—and teen helpers—as they could find.

When she saw the grateful and enthusiastic response of the parents, Trudy started having second thoughts about leaving for vacation. Monica promised to record as much of the event as possible on her camcorder and told Trudy to go. Though Pastor Fenner had never hosted a Camp Comeback, he assured Lloyd and Trudy he'd survived more day camps and vacation Bible schools than he could count. "Anyway," he reminded Trudy, "you and your team have this so organized that there isn't anything for me to do except show up and listen to the kids sing their songs."

Getting away turned out to be "just the ticket." Lloyd and Trudy were delighted with the beach condo, the leisurely walks on the beach, the time spent helping the boys build sand castles, and above all, the breathing space just to be away from disaster sights and sounds. The two of them returned from their spring-break family vacation resolved to do a better job of taking care of themselves and to get away more often. While they had enjoyed themselves and the play time with the boys, they had also realized how totally exhausted they were from the stress. Their first Sunday back, they sat together as a family while Pastor Rick Fenner presided at morning worship.

That Monday the two pastors spent the entire afternoon talking about how Pastor Fenner could be most helpful to Emanuel, Lloyd, and the Caldwell community. They decided, given that everyone was still in recovery mode, just to take it week by week. For the coming week Rick would focus on visiting members in their homes or workplaces, so they'd feel more comfortable coming to him for pastoral care later. Lloyd would preach and try to do a little planning for the upcoming Easter season.

"I've been wondering what all this means for Emanuel and our community in the long term," Lloyd confided. "Before I committed to taking this break, I was thinking it was time for me to move on. But I'd hate to leave now. I'd feel that I was abandoning my people when the ship was sinking. But I wasn't trained for disaster response. I just don't know how to organize myself or my people for all the changes we're up against. And the depression—I try to be upbeat and to trust God, but it's much harder than I thought it would be."

"That's why I'm here, my friend. I can see how heavy a load all of you carry. I can't do much to make the circumstances better, but I can sure walk with you through it. I was so proud of my people when I talked to them about the possibility of coming back for an extended stay. They pretty much said, 'Why are you asking? Of course you should go.' Then our retired friend showed up—not knowing anything about this situation—to ask if she could help. It all just fell into place."

"There's a question I keep trying to answer—because so many people ask me one way or another."

"What's that?" asked Rick.

"Why do you think terrible things like this flood happen? I mean, I've studied the problem of pain and evil, as I know you have. But really, there's nothing in our theology that answers that question."

"We could debate the various theories people have offered through the ages. But you and I both know that wouldn't really help."

"But it might help to offer some sort of class on it," Lloyd said, thinking aloud.

"Maybe. And if you like, I'll work up something on that. Ultimately, I guess we just aren't supposed to know. Look at Job. In the end, he just had to trust."

"Yeah, I guess so," Lloyd said. "And Joseph. His brothers meant it for evil when they stuffed him in the pit, but God used it for good when Joseph became second in command in Egypt. But that doesn't explain floods and fires and other pestilence."

"No, of course it doesn't. But maybe we're not supposed to figure out why. Maybe we're just invited to decide how . . . how we'll respond when others suffer. How we'll prepare ourselves for the inevitable storms of life. What we'll focus on when we walk through disasters."

"I've been thinking a lot about that," Lloyd said. "I've been thinking about what Emanuel ought to be like a year from now."

"You think you need a new mission?"

"Yes, I do. We've been blown away, not by the storm—though that too—but by people like you. It's unbelievable what people have done for us. People who probably never knew there was a Caldwell here. People who have their own problems and messes to clean up."

"Sounds like you've been doing some long-range thinking along with your long-term recovery work."

Lloyd was quiet for a moment. Then he said, "You know, I think maybe I have part of the answer about the why."

"And the answer is . . . ?"

"Though it's true we've been hurt badly, and will be in recovery for a long time, it's just as true that we've been blessed. Maybe we have a mission now to figure out how to be a blessing to others trying to recovery from a disaster."

"If that's so, you won't run out of work anytime soon," said Rick. "It's a mess out there. Not just from storms like your community had, but from all kinds of storms—some natural, some caused by all sorts of out-of-control human acts of insanity."

"Thanks for listening, Rick. Now I know why you're here. I need you to help pick up the slack, so I can start working with my members on our plans for the future."

"Whatever I can do, my friend. Whatever I can do."

A Decision to Make

Should Emmanuel make disaster response part of its long-term mission?

How a congregation or a community recovers from a disaster depends on the nature of the disaster, how extensive the damage, and the likelihood of a similar disaster in the future. In the case of Emanuel, the damage to the buildings was minor, but the impact on the area served by the congregation was extensive. Before the storm, the congregation had been focused on upgrading facilities and expanding programming for the growing number of younger families moving into the area.

Since the storm Lloyd and various leaders of the congregation had discussed a different set of priorities. They were now putting more focus on passing on some of the help they'd been receiving for the past six months. Hardly a week went by that someone didn't stop to share a story about some random act of kindness recently witnessed. Lloyd was hearing similar stories from his colleagues around town, too.

Emanuel's leaders were thinking that maybe their facilities were adequate for the time being. Maybe the funds they'd raised in their recent campaign would be better spent underwriting the cost for some of their members to go help out in other disaster areas. When Lloyd broached the subject with the DPR team, most members wanted to explore what they could do for others, once they were through the worst of their own recovery work. They decided to host a one-day congregational retreat with any members who wanted to participate in the discussion. The agenda for the retreat would be simple. They would ask people how the storm had changed their priorities. The question would be: "Should we (Emanuel) make disaster-response outreach part of our long-term focus?"

Yes. It makes sense to apply all the new knowledge.

- Receiving the many out-of-town guest volunteer workers had done so much to boost morale and inspire the members of Emanuel that they wanted to be on the giving end of the recovery process for others.
- Most people were unaware of how disaster-response ministry worked before they experienced their own disaster. Now that they knew about this incredible ministry, they wouldn't feel right not doing something to help others struggling with recovery issues.
- As volunteers constantly thanked Emanuel members for allowing them to help and told how the volunteer ministry made such a positive impact on their congregations back home, the members realized it really could be more of a blessing to give than to receive.

No. We have too much work to do right here.

- It would be a long time before Caldwell and Green County were fully recovered. There was too much work to be done at home.
- The disaster had made people more aware of just how many in their own community were living with low-grade disasters of various sorts before the storm. They would do well to focus on dealing with local needs. These included unemployment and underemployment, inadequate and inferior housing and schools, lack of affordable medical care for low-income families, and other social issues that kept local residents in a constant state of frustration and discouragement.
- While all who had come into contact with the disaster volunteers were touched and inspired by their generosity, most

people were still feeling too weighed down by their own losses to envision getting organized to volunteer in another region of the country.

- The campaign had raised money for facilities. It wouldn't be proper to change goals after the money was pledged for that purpose.

Maybe. It doesn't have to be all or nothing.

- It wouldn't have to be an all-or-nothing commitment. Emanuel's members could scale back their remodeling plans and earmark a portion of their funds for disaster-recovery efforts—with approval from those making the pledges.
- They could set up a special appeal fund, sponsoring only as many volunteers as the fund could cover. When the fund ran out of money, individuals would have to pay their own way to volunteer.
- They could work with their denomination's disaster-response organization to determine the most critical needs. Perhaps they could underwrite one or more of these outreach programs every year while still eventually doing their own upgrade projects.

What You Need to Know about . . .

INCREASING RESILIENCY AMONG DISASTER SURVIVORS

Everyone experiences setbacks of some sort once in a while. How quickly and fully a person recovers from the setback and moves on to a new chapter of life with vitality and hope is influenced by many factors. Research with survivors of many types of calamities—including natural disasters, wars, domestic violence, severe illness, major accidents, and job-related losses—indicates variables that compassionate people can influence. Some of these variables are called "assets." Though an individual's attitude, beliefs, and values are key factors in recovery, so too is the climate or culture in which the individual lives.

1. Social scientists doing research on how children develop resiliency—that is, the ability to overcome obstacles and appropriately develop their potential—have identified certain factors that maximize a child's likelihood of success. These factors or life circumstances are known as "assets." In this context an asset is a personal circumstance or characteristic that enables an individual to limit self-destructive behaviors and pursue pro-active ones. For example:

   - The individual has regular contact with three or more caring adults who show interest in his or her activities and interests.
   - Parents consider school studies important and support them in a variety of ways—creating time and space to study, helping with homework drills, reviewing reports, attending school functions.
   - The individual is part of a cohesive and emotionally healthy social network of friends and peers at school, youth groups, clubs, neighborhood playmates, and so forth.

2. Social scientists have tracked the impact of both the presence and absence of these assets. They find a strong correlation between assets and overall functioning. That is, the more assets an individual has, the fewer negative behaviors he or she engages in—such as addictions, stealing, casual sexual encounters, violence, and the like.
3. The reverse correlation also holds true. The fewer assets an individual has, the more likely he or she is to engage in negative behaviors.
4. Whole families, congregations, and communities also function along a continuum of health based on similar asset principles.

For example, a community with effective, cohesive leadership in place before a disaster will be much more likely to recover fully and sooner than a community struggling with corrupt, indecisive, or divisive leadership.

5. Congregations and communities can strengthen existing assets and instill new assets through education, strong leadership, cooperative efforts, and creative thinking.
6. One important component of good disaster-preparedness work is to make an inventory of a congregation's strengths and to develop ways to rely on these strengths in a disaster. For example, perhaps one of a congregation's passions and strengths is to gather frequently for fellowship. This practice should be resumed as soon as possible after a disaster to provide a place for people to support one another. If a congregation is known for its outstanding worship services, then worship could be a source of comfort and encouragement as people seek to be in touch with God in their time of sorrow and struggle. A congregation that has a well-developed and effective youth-ministry program can help stabilize the social structures for youth who have lost their schools or other important social outlets as a result of disaster.

Implications for Your Congregation

People naturally turn to their congregations for support and encouragement during both individual and community-wide challenges. Knowing this, congregational leaders can increase their effectiveness in a time of need by thinking about their congregation's "assets" or strengths during times of calm.

- Take time at a congregational meeting or council retreat or education forum to have members list the top three strengths of your congregation. Combine individual responses into a congregational list.

- How might these strengths be helpful in a disaster recovery?
- A disaster leaves behind many issues—far too many for any one congregation to handle. By taking time to identify what your congregation does best, you also help avoid the trap of trying to do too much for too many for too long.
- Partnerships are the key to community long-term recovery. Think of the process as a kind of potluck supper. When each congregation adds what it has to offer to the community recovery effort, the whole is greater than the sum of the parts. How can your congregation partner with other congregations in your community?

Strangers No More

After the attacks on the World Trade Center in New York on September 11, 2001, one congregation used that event as the starting point for regular dialogues with Muslim neighbors who were members of a nearby mosque. They wanted to understand one another's cultures better and to send a message of reconciliation and peace between diverse groups rather than allowing fear and ignorance to dominate the reaction to the disaster.

Resources

Search Institute, "40 Developmental Assets"; *www.search-institute.org*. Search Institute is devoted to research on factors that foster emotionally healthy youth and families.

Mary Lynn Pulley and Michael Wakefield, ***Building Resiliency: How to Thrive in Times of Change*** (Greensboro, N.C.: Center for Creative Leadership, 2001). Nine developmental components that increase ability to adapt to the unknown.

Questions for Reflection

1. What are some of your favorite getaway places when you feel overwhelmed or pressured by the demands of life?
2. What are some ways you can create a stress-free zone in your home? In your workplace?
3. Who are the people in your circle of family and close friends who may need additional support should a disaster occur? How might you or your congregation help provide that support?
4. Think of your life when you were a preteen. What was your family life like? What was your school life like? Describe your neighborhood. How do you think your life would be different if you were a preteen in your community today?
5. If a family member living far away from you needed help, what options would you have for getting help for that person without going to the rescue yourself?

Scripture Reflection

Rejoice in the Lord always. I will say it again: Rejoice! Let your gentleness be evident to all. The Lord is near. Do not be anxious about anything, but in everything, by prayer and petition, with thanksgiving, present your requests to God. And the peace of God, which transcends all understanding, will guard your hearts and your minds in Christ Jesus.

—Philippians 4:4–7

CHAPTER 11

A Future with Hope

CONGREGATIONAL LIFE AFTER A DISASTER

"For I know the plans I have for you," declares the Lord,
"plans to prosper you and not to harm you,
plans to give you hope and a future."
—Jeremiah 29:11

Timeline

The summer after the storm, approaching the one-year anniversary of the flood. Through a series of in-home gatherings, Emanuel leaders have collected feedback from nearly two-thirds of the members. The vast majority of the feedback affirms the concept of refocusing congregational efforts on outreach to others in disaster areas. They decide to host a one-day congregational planning event the weekend before the one-year anniversary of the storm.

Situation

Lloyd and Evelyn were mulling over how to handle the one-year anniversary worship service at Emanuel. They'd been through so much in the past eleven months. In some ways it seemed as though the storm had never happened. Parish life had slowly gotten back to a manageable routine of administrative and pastoral details. Many members of the congregation, however, were still dealing with disaster-recovery issues. Others were now actively engaged in various disaster-recovery volunteer projects. For still others, the storm was long gone, and they were thinking about other things these days.

Sadly, a few families were no longer in Caldwell. They had lost their jobs because of the flood, and they could not find new ones in the post-disaster economic slump. Emanuel received a few new members as a result of hosting the Camp Comeback program last spring. Grateful families who had no church home decided to give the church a try. Their children felt right at home after spending a week there for the camp, and the parents soon did too.

Lloyd still attended the Saturday breakfasts whenever he could. The group had slowly dwindled down to the faithful few, but those who stayed with it had forged deep friendships and partnerships. They commented frequently how grateful they were for one another's support through the post-storm recovery chapter of their lives. Lloyd told Trudy that he had always hoped doing parish ministry would be this collegial, but until they started leaning on one another, he'd given up on actually experiencing such close cooperation.

The group decided to hold a massive outdoor anniversary event at a park along the now-tranquil Green River. The flood had all but destroyed the park, but hardworking volunteers had restored it. They'd replaced the washed-out picnic tables, removed mountains of flood debris, built and installed new playground equipment, and completed other cleanup jobs. Service clubs in the area had raised money for a memorial for the park. It was dedicated to the many volunteers who had come to their aid in the wake of the storm. There was some talk around town of renaming it "Volunteer Park."

Long-term Memory

Halifax, Nova Scotia, suffered a terrible explosion during World War I. On December 6, 1917, two ships collided in its harbor. One of the vessels, a French cargo ship, was carrying ammunition for the war effort in Europe and exploded, killing an estimated two thousand people, and injuring nine thousand in the resulting fires and collapsed buildings. A train left Boston that same night,

> carrying doctors, nurses, and other medical personnel, as well as desperately needed supplies. A winter snowstorm slowed its progress, but it arrived thirty hours later, at 3:00 A.M. on December 8. As a way of remembering the help from the Boston Red Cross and other civic groups, the City of Halifax has sent the City of Boston a Christmas tree every year since 1971. The tree is carefully selected and is put on display on Boston Common. It's the way one city says to another city, "Thanks for the help in our time of need; we've never forgotten your generosity."

After the positive feedback from the Camp Comeback project over spring break, Trudy started making regular contact with one of the designers of the camp curriculum. That led to an invitation to attend a regional conference for educators who worked with grade-school youth. At the conference Trudy attended a workshop on how adults could help children acquire the resources they needed to develop resiliency. The presenters focused on how important it was for congregations, schools, and others who work with youth to partner to provide an environment in which children could gain these resources. Workshop presenters urged participants to think of themselves as asset-builders, people who collectively surrounded youth with healthy environments in which to grow. Trudy returned energized and determined to launch an assets-based initiative in Caldwell. Jackie was interested in helping her. So was Monica. The three soon started referring to themselves as the "Three Musketeers of Assets." They were gradually growing a network of interested parents, teachers, youth workers, and grandparents. They were looking to host a workshop to explain the concepts and to solicit funds to bring the program into the school system of Caldwell. Trudy's work as an assistant principal gave her the needed credibility and contacts.

The Emanuel DPR team continued to meet once a month. At the most recent meeting they had taken time to evaluate what worked well and what didn't in their first disaster. Jill Hanson was proud of the effort they had made, and grateful for what they'd had in place before the flood. However, they all agreed they couldn't just let this be one more "been there, done that" experience in life. They wanted to keep the need for disaster preparation in front of people. Most of their monthly meetings were dedicated to developing fact sheets for congregations and individual households to use for their disaster-preparation planning.

All the lay members of the team had unintentionally become disaster consultants where they worked. Hal Beckman was now officially part of the Green County Hospital's disaster-management team. Sometimes he marveled how God had led him out of the flooded land of his previous home in Louisiana, to Caldwell and another flood, and now to helping others prepare for future disasters. His hospital position provided him access to a wealth of disaster-response resources. His experience of living through two floods in three years gave him a passion to help others with disaster issues. His work was becoming more and more focused on such issues. He realized how valuable his telecommunications knowledge was to the overall disaster management effort.

Faith Monroe's significant contributions to the Red Cross shelter effort resulted in an invitation for her to join the staff of the regional Red Cross office. She was surprised at how she thrived on being around people whose lives were in total chaos. She was frequently gone on weekends to various conferences or recovery sites, but the energy and excitement she had as a result of this work made that a small price to pay.

Monica and her family were pretty well settled into their remodeled home, which they referred to as their "mandatory remodeling project." Between managing the preschool and working with Trudy and Jackie on the new assets initiative, she was busier than ever. The preschool was heading into some serious financial trouble. Lacy Rogers, the congregation's finance committee chair, issued grim reports and reminders of the financial crisis at Emanuel's monthly council meetings. Monica had reluctantly ended the policy of letting any child whose family had been directly affected by the storm attend at no or low tuition. It tore at her maternal instincts to turn down a child whose parents couldn't pay for tuition. She hoped the assets work might lead to a grant to build up a scholarship fund.

Cindy Henderson had decided that her retirement focus would be grant-proposal writing. Everywhere she looked around Caldwell she saw another problem that required funding to solve. She took time out to attend a grant-writing class in Yorkshire. Now she was offering her services to the various local nonprofit organizations that had been formed in response to the storm.

As members of Emanuel and the entire Green County area approached the storm's one-year anniversary, people wanted to look back on the progress they'd made. They also wanted to look forward to what life might be like in the coming year. The attendance at Emanuel's one-day "Future of Hope" retreat surprised everyone. The fellowship area was packed with more than one hundred people—all eager to hear what their congregational leaders had to say and to render their own opinions. Lloyd opened with a devotion based on Jeremiah 29: "For surely I know the plans I have for you, says the LORD, plans for your welfare and not for harm, to give you a future with hope" (Jer. 29:11 NRSV).

"Well, what a difference a year makes!" Lloyd said. "Do you remember when this room was the living room for our Red Cross guests? And the kitchen was in full operation, minus electricity—cranking out three meals a day? And when we hosted the weekly 'Welcome to Our Disaster' Sunday-evening dinners for the volunteers? We've all been through so much. It's too much to summarize, and yet it's too significant not to talk about. What we want to talk about today is the answer to this question: 'Now what?'

"Where do we, as a congregation, go from here? We can't go back to life the way it was before the storm. That was a pretty good life for many of us, but we can't go back. Do we postpone our long-range plans to stay focused on local recovery efforts? There's still much to do. There are buildings to rehab; there are workers to help retool, so that they can find better jobs; there are social-service efforts to support. As we learned so well with our Camp Comeback kids, there are *many* families right here in Green County who need a lot of support and encouragement to get beyond this tragedy in their lives.

"As we've also learned from the many workers—paid and volunteer—who have poured into our community, disasters bring out the best and the worst we have to offer to one another. Haven't the volunteers been terrific?" This question was answered with a round of applause.

Lloyd wondered whether his members would be as upset as he had been upon learning that some itinerant contract workers had been victimized by unscrupulous employers. "But we also know that many hardworking hourly-wage earners came from far away only to become another group of victimized people—victimized not by the storm itself but by dishonest people looking to make a profit off the situation. Workers were promised a place to stay and three hundred dollars a day to help reroof houses and remove storm debris. In far too many cases, these promises weren't kept. Some workers were never paid at all. Others had to spend most of what they earned on meals and inadequate and overcrowded housing.

"The storm has made us look at the substandard housing too many of our residents have to call 'home.' Hundreds of people displaced as property owners declare bankruptcy and let their flooded buildings slowly rot. Maybe we will want to address some of these problems. Some out-of-state property owners have refused to make any repairs. It's a blight on our community and a travesty for the poor tenants who are stuck in these rat traps.

"However, we all know we'd never be as far along the recovery road as we are if it hadn't been for the hundreds of men, women, and youth who came week after week—and who are still coming. What would we have done without Pastor Fenner and his people? Maybe we will want to pass on to others what we've received from them. It's for you to decide."

Over the course of the next few hours, the people worked in small groups around tables to hammer out their vision of what it would mean to be a people who helped create a future with hope for other people. At the end of the day they handed in their notes and worksheets. The congregation put together a joint planning team, consisting of a few DPR team members as well as a few church council members. This group collected the notes to refer to as they worked on a proposal for the congregation's future. The draft was then printed in the church newsletter, posted on bulletin boards, placed on the congregation's website, and inserted in the worship bulletins for several weeks. On the Sunday before the one-year anniversary of the storm, Emanuel held a brief congregational meeting to ratify this Future of Hope proposal.

The one-year anniversary of the flood fell on a Thursday. It was a crystal-clear day with a Wedgwood-blue sky and warm temperatures. It was the kind of day when everyone wanted to find an excuse to be outside. The excuse was the community service at Green River Park. People brought lawn chairs and blankets. Nearly every religious leader in town had a part in the service. A fifty-voice community choir sang. Seemingly every child or teen in town who had ever played a musical instrument was in the community orchestra. Those who came were amazed and touched to see Jack Shaffer, the FEMA staff member, and many others who came from out of town, both to remember what had happened and to acknowledge the progress that had been made.

The two-hour service that afternoon was filled with prayers of thanks for God's faithfulness, and gratitude for the hundreds who had come to help the community recover. The same woman who spoke at the first community service, Clara Longstreth, spoke again. The passing year had been hard on her. She was in a wheelchair now. Her voice was soft, but with the help of a microphone she managed to deliver her message of encouragement to the silent congregation. "My eyes have seen the glory of the coming of the Lord," she whispered into the microphone. "My Lord has come here again and again. Through you. Though I didn't think I'd live through that horrible storm, I did. And I'm sure glad for it. I will die a happy woman now, for I've seen the goodness and mercy of God, and if you haven't—well, you just haven't been looking. God's certainly been with us this year."

People stayed and mingled after the service until dusk, when the mosquitoes finally persuaded them to head home.

Lloyd and Trudy tucked their boys into bed and went to their favorite chairs in the family room. They sat in silence for a long time. Finally Lloyd said, "I wouldn't wish what this disaster did to our people on my worst enemy. But I wouldn't have missed for anything seeing the way our people have come together. I don't know why it takes a disaster to get us to realize how much we need each other. But by golly—we sure do have a lot of great people who have gone a lot of extra miles this past year. Trudy, I don't know when I've been so proud of my church and these people."

"Amen to that, brother," she grinned at him. "The future does look bright. The road ahead is still pretty rocky, but together we'll make it. Haven't we learned a lot about how to support one another this past year?"

"Indeed we have."

"What next?"

"Well, we have a pretty clear mandate on three fronts. We keep on keeping on as best we can at Emanuel. I like the idea of getting all who are willing to write up their stories and publish them in a little booklet. Seems a perfect project for Helen to tackle. I've already talked to her."

"Let me guess. She said yes."

"Right you are. As usual."

"And the other two?"

"Some of our folks are chomping at the bit, so to speak, to work on some issues here in Green County. I'm not sure I can hold them back. I'll work with my Saturday breakfast gang on ways to do that."

"And?"

"And it doesn't seem quite right to be waiting for a disaster to strike so that our volunteers can go help someone else, but there are quite a few who are ready, willing, and I believe more than a little able to go where they are needed. We're going to bring down a couple of disaster-organization staff people to lead a volunteer training event, so they'll be ready to go when needed."

"Could you ever have imagined any of this a year ago?"

"No, I could not. But now the future looks pretty good. God really does bring good out of evil and joy out of mourning."

"Here's to a future with hope," said Trudy. She and Lloyd raised their coffee mugs and tapped them together as their way of saying "Amen."

Two Decisions to Make

First, will you, dear reader, make it a priority to think through what you, your family, and your faith family need to do to prepare as best you can for a disaster? That task is the best starting place to get involved in disaster-recovery ministry.

Secondly, will you commit to helping others recover when they encounter a disaster? See appendix I for more information about the impact of disaster-response work on organizations both large and small.

When we hear the term "disaster," most of us probably think of a destructive storm, fire, earthquake, volcano, blizzard, or other natural event. Or perhaps we imagine a calamity of human origin, such as war or mass shootings or intentional destruction of property and murder of innocent bystanders. For sure, these are the kinds of disasters that require the services of trained professionals. Their work is supplemented with the efforts of volunteers. However, you don't have to wait for one of these mega-events to strike to find people trying to cope with the aftermath of disaster.

An economic downturn, a wave of drug-induced domestic violence, an illicit business that enslaves others to make a profit—all leave behind victims. Anywhere and everywhere you look through the eyes of faith and compassion, you will find others in need of support to recover from a tragedy.

God promises to be with us always—in all ways—to the end of time. The way that God honors that promise is by nudging ordinary men and women to respond to the needs around them. Disaster response ultimately boils down to some very basic principles:

Find a need, and fill it.

See a person in pain, and console him or her.

Start where you are. Use what resources you have. Just do what you can.

We cannot know when a disaster will come our way. We cannot predict what the nature of the disaster will be. We cannot know how the disaster will affect our loved ones and our communities. But this we do know: God promises to be with us through any disaster. We can prepare. We can decide to respond as needed. We can trust that by the grace of God and the compassionate support of one another, we can recover.

Additional Resources

Kathleen Smith, ***Stilling the Storm: Worship and Congregational Leadership in Difficult Times*** (Herndon, Va.: Alban Institute, 2006).

Peter L. Steinke, ***Congregational Leadership in Anxious Times: Being Calm and Courageous No Matter What*** (Herndon, Va.: Alban Institute, 2006).

Questions for Reflection

1. Describe some events in your life that seemed hopeless but ultimately opened the door to a new opportunity.
2. Who are some of the most optimistic people you know? What do you think makes them this way?
3. Do you know any people with an amazing turnaround story—people who have overcome incredible obstacles to obtain a good outcome?

4. What situations draw out the passion in you?
5. What situations draw out the *com*passion in you?

Scripture Reflection

But those who hope in the L*ORD*
will renew their strength.
They will soar on wings like eagles;
they will run and not grow weary,
they will walk and not be faint.
—Isaiah 40:31

CHAPTER 12

Justice, Kindness, and Walking Humbly

WHY ENGAGE IN DISASTER RESPONSE?

He has told you, O mortal, what is good;
and what does the Lord *require of you*
but to do justice, and to love kindness,
and to walk humbly with your God?
—Micah 6:8 NRSV

Timeline

One year and following after the disaster. Most people of Green County have moved forward and into their "new normal" lives after the disaster. It has become only one part of their life story. New relationships have been formed, and many old "business as usual" aspects of day-to-day life have been forever changed. Sadly, some have not yet been able to move on and seem stuck in their recovery. Some may never recover. It is for these people that the work of the faith community goes on.

Disaster Response as a Calling

Disaster work is both fulfilling and challenging. The small successes and the "warm fuzzy" moments are many. The potential for seeing the fruits of one's labor is great. When done well, disaster-response service evokes cooperation at amazingly high levels. At the same time, the realization that the work is never done, or that it will be quickly undone by the next disaster, can be disheartening. The challenges of working with conflicting philosophies and competing agendas can make even the savviest politician tremble. And, as in many areas of public life, the funds and resources are never sufficient to meet the need.

So why do we do it? For some, disaster work meets a personal need. It provides an adrenaline fix that keeps the "disaster junkie" moving from one site to the next, thriving on the chaos and soaking up the drama and trauma of the moment. For others, it is a job. Responding to disasters is what puts food on the family table and a roof over their heads. If not their full-time work, it comes with the territory of the career they have chosen. But for the vast majority of those in the field, disaster work fills the mandate laid out in Micah 6:8: "Do justice, love kindness, and walk humbly." It is the core of who they are called to be in the world.

Disaster preparation and response, done well, exemplify human community the way God intended it to be. It rises above our imposed borders and classifications and brings us together to solve human problems in unique and collaborative ways. It can move us out of our comfortable places within the cozy walls of our churches or synagogues or mosques and into the larger community where God's people are hurting. This work can help us define what it truly means to be people of God.

Do Justice

As the good people of Emanuel and Caldwell discovered, disaster has a way of washing to the surface issues in the community that would otherwise be ignored by the general population—poverty, inadequate housing, unemployment or underemployment, and homelessness, to name a few. Micah calls us, as people of God, to tend to the vulnerable and to seek justice within the community. Disaster work often provides the catalyst for communities to focus on these issues.

One stage of the disaster cycle is mitigation. While often a part of preparation, mitigation is more than preparation. Mitigation is tending to those things that will make the effects of any disaster less disastrous. Mitigation seeks to stabilize homes against floods or hurricanes or earthquakes. Mitigation is helping vulnerable populations understand the value of saving for a "rainy day." Mitigation is working with city planners to allow for adequate flood control and managed development that protect all citizens. The mitigation stage of disaster response is exactly what Micah calls for when he tells us to seek justice.

The disaster response itself gives the people of God many opportunities to seek justice. The recovery process will repeatedly lift up the "least of these" as the people affected seek to restore their lives. Many residents fall through the cracks or are overlooked in communities eager to get life moving forward again. Faith communities are called to keep advocating on behalf of those whose voices are not heard or whose plight goes unseen. Doing justice is imperative in faithful disaster preparedness and response.

Down but Not Out

After the disaster, Sheila eventually lost everything except her life and the clothes she was wearing. First she lost her home, job, community, and car. She and her husband evacuated and couldn't return home. The apartment complex in which they had lived was condemned. Her workplace was too damaged to open after the hurricane. The community college she had been attending was closed indefinitely. Her extended family members had all lived within a few miles of each other before the disaster. After the disaster they were scattered over several states, living in FEMA housing. Sheila and her husband evacuated in her husband's truck. Her own car had been destroyed by the disaster. Within six months she also lost her husband, who couldn't deal with all the losses, and abandoned her—but not before she had become pregnant with their first child.

Stranded in a new city, separated from everything and everyone that was familiar, and carrying her first baby, Sheila was determined to find a way to start over. She decided the first step was to get a car so that she could get to the doctor, look for work, and start the long journey toward self-sufficiency for herself and her soon-to-be-born son.

However, since she couldn't provide any paperwork for the car—or any evidence that the car had been destroyed—she couldn't get financial aid to replace it. For several frustrating months she tried to work through the system to get together enough money to replace the car. Finally she turned to the church. It took many months, but eventually a handful of people worked with her to meet her need for reliable transportation. Pulling their resources together, a group of twenty-five people contributed gifts ranging from a few dollars to a few hundred dollars each and raised enough to buy a good used vehicle. One couple found a used van in excellent condition at a low price. It had high mileage, but it passed a mechanic's rigorous inspection with flying colors.

Right before Christmas, Sheila was given the van and the help she needed to get it registered and licensed. Shortly after that, she and her new son, Victor, moved into the FEMA housing offered her in yet another new community. This time she would be living in a home in a small rural community near a major city—where she could easily find work, child care, and college classes—as long as she had a car.

Disasters result in catastrophe for thousands of people like Sheila who need a little boost to get over the many roadblocks that impede their full recovery. Doing justice often means removing barriers.

Love Kindness

When disaster hits, it strikes at the core of people's daily lives. It rattles routines and shakes foundational beliefs about the world and life. Simple tasks become difficult. Things that one previously accomplished without thinking about them now require monumental effort. No longer can one just stop for a gallon of milk on the way home from work. Is the grocery store even open? If it is, will it have milk? If it does, will you have enough ice at home to keep it cool? How long will it take to get home with the traffic lights out? Is the route you usually take even open yet?

Priorities shift, and daily life focuses on the basics, on sheer survival. In the midst of this upheaval, Micah reminds us to "love kindness." Far too often in disaster response, kindness is confused with the individual's need to "fix things" or to offer up answers to the inevitable "Why?" Well-meaning responders interpret kindness as doing for others what they are capable of doing themselves. Others may think that kindness means shielding people from pain or reality. These seem to be compassionate behaviors but in fact impede healing.

True kindness understands that no one has the answers. True kindness acts without judgment or prejudice. True kindness does not seek to condemn or convert. True kindness is reaching out to touch a hurting person. It is a hot cup of coffee amid the chaos of a FEMA POD. It is standing next to a family as they survey the remains of their home, or helping them carry out what's left of their furniture. Kindness is walking alongside rather than in front of or behind the hurting person. Disaster-response ministry provides ample opportunity for God's people to practice Micah's command to love kindness.

Open Windows

Darrel wasn't much interested in "church stuff," but he wasn't going to let his work friend—Harry—go alone to see his flooded house for the first time. The two of them had trouble getting inside. The muddy muck was several inches deep throughout the house, so the front and back doors were impossible to push open.

They tried the windows. One window in the kitchen was unlocked, and they crawled through it. Harry stood by the overturned kitchen table in shock. He tried to comprehend the magnitude of both

> the loss and the work to be done. Not knowing what else to do or say, Darrel started sorting through the muck in search of anything salvageable. He spotted a corner of a small ceramic plaque poking up through the mud. He nearly dropped it when he pulled it out and read the words inscribed on it: "When God closes a door, he opens a window."
>
> Harry turned to see Darrel holding the plaque with his mouth open in awe. "I think there may be something to this God business after all," he said. "Maybe I could go to church with you one of these Sundays."
>
> Disaster-response ministry is full of such moments for those willing to engage in acts of kindness.

Walk Humbly

Micah reminds us that the work of God's people is not about who gets the credit or who gets the gold star for doing it "right." God's work is best accomplished when we are able to put aside our own personal or denominational agendas and focus on caring for those in need. This shift happens in disaster-response ministry as a matter of course. It is not unusual that in the midst of a disaster response, one may find the Seventh-day Adventists transporting supplies collected, boxed, and stored by the Latter Day Saints for use at a Lutheran church's overnight shelter. This kind of cooperation is the work of God's community at its best.

Unfortunately, it is also not uncommon to see people of faith losing sight of the command to "walk humbly." Often congregations and faith-based organizations get caught up in the need to make sure that *their* work is recognized in the community. Or they become convinced that no one else is doing it quite right, and they venture out on their own. When this happens, the power of the combined community is diluted. The strengths that the faith community brings to the recovery are truly realized only when we are all able to "walk humbly" in our work.

Divine Error

A small crew was sent by Presbyterian Disaster Response to muck out a home in New Orleans. The elderly couple who greeted the team members thanked them over and over as they hauled mud-soaked household furnishings to the curb. At the end of the day the team leader showed the couple the team's work orders for the next day and asked for directions to the house that was to be their next assignment.

The man and woman stared at each other and started weeping. Confused, the team leader waited patiently for them to compose themselves. Eventually the man spoke. "You aren't at the right address. This isn't the house on your list for today."

"Well," said the team leader. "You needed the help, so that's OK."

"No, no, you don't understand," explained the woman. "We were so discouraged. There's no way we could deal with all this at our age. We decided last night that if something didn't change today, we were going to take all our medicines and be done with all . . . ." Her voice trailed off, and she couldn't finish the story. But the team leader understood she meant that they would have committed suicide rather than continue under such difficult circumstances.

"Then I guess we were at the right address after all," he said as he gave each of them a hug and wished them well.

Disaster recovery work is very much God-work. The role of responders is to be open to letting God decide when and where and how our services are needed.

So why do we do it? Why do we engage in the often messy, back-aching, heart-breaking, painful, yet rewarding and exhilarating work of disaster response? The answer is simple. As people of faith, we can do no less.

APPENDIX A

Red Cross Sheltering

In 1905 the American Red Cross was granted a charter by the United States government to provide several services on its behalf:

- To "carry on a system of national and international relief in time of peace and to apply the same in mitigating the sufferings caused by pestilence, famine, fire, floods, and other great national calamities."
- To devise means for preventing disasters and "to promote measures of humanity and welfare of mankind."

It is under this charter that the American Red Cross works with government agencies to provide sheltering operations during and after a disaster. While every disaster is different, the following are some general operating principles to expect when considering offering a church building or other facility as a Red Cross shelter.

- The Red Cross will either pay for or reimburse any expenses incurred by a congregation as a result of opening a shelter. These include (but may not be limited to) food, utilities, and damage to buildings.
- The Red Cross also covers all liability associated with the shelter and will absorb any legal costs that may arise.
- In general, a facility offered as a shelter needs to be safe and comfortable, and to provide a secure area where shelter residents

can sleep and eat. Kitchens and showers are preferred but not necessary.

- The Red Cross will work with a congregation to determine how many people the facility can house, looking at a variety of factors, including square footage.
- The Red Cross does not support animals (except service animals) in shelters but seeks to partner with other organizations to find safe spaces for pets during a disaster.
- The Red Cross does not discriminate in who is allowed to reside in a shelter. The first goal is to keep all people safe. Be aware that this policy means that a congregation may become a temporary home to people with a broad range of social or personal problems such as being homeless or having undiagnosed mental-health issues.
- Red Cross shelter staff and volunteers are not expected to be able to tend to specialized medical needs. However, any person with special medical needs who is either self-sufficient or accompanied by a caregiver who can provide adequate care is welcome to stay in a shelter. People with special medical needs cannot assume that a shelter will have any specialized equipment beyond basic first-aid supplies.

Keep in mind that each situation is unique. The local Red Cross chapter will work with a congregation to explore the feasibility of using its facilities as a shelter. For more information or to locate the nearest American Red Cross chapter, visit *www.redcross.org*.

APPENDIX B

Emergency Kits

The American Red Cross website (*www.redcross.org*) provides excellent resources about how to prepare for a disaster and what to pack in an emergency kit; it even offers a basic kit for less than twenty dollars. What you will need in your kit depends, of course, on where you live and whom you're living with, but here are some basics.

- Sturdy plastic storage bins with tight-fitting covers in which to store emergency kit items.
- A gallon of water per person for a minimum of three days. (Don't forget about your pets.)
- Protective outerwear appropriate for the climate.
- Blankets for cold weather; battery-operated fans for hot weather.
- Flashlights (with spare batteries), lanterns, light sticks, or candles (and matches).
- Facemasks to prevent inhaling mold and toxic chemicals.
- Work gloves to wear when removing debris; plastic gloves to protect hands from toxins.
- Hand-sanitizer gel.
- Whistle and neck cord.
- An ax to cut through a roof, break out a window, or clear fallen tree limbs.
- First-aid kit with Band-Aids, antiseptic cream, alcohol wipes, and other basic necessities.

- Sufficient food items that require no cooking or refrigeration—enough for three days for each person (and food for your pets).
- Cash. Determine what you consider a necessary daily allowance for each person in your family, multiply that by a minimum of seven days—and keep that amount of cash stored in your emergency kit. Factor in the possibility that you may have to pay cash for gasoline for a while.
- Copies of critical documents such as birth and marriage certificates, proof of insurance, and "in case of emergency" ("ICE") contact information for family members and close friends who do not live with you.
- Plastic bags of various sizes—small to store leftover food, medium to store wet clothing or dirty laundry, large to contain litter and debris.
- Appropriate clothing for your climate, but regardless of climate, sturdy, closed-toed shoes to protect your feet, long-sleeved shirts, and slacks or jeans to protect from abrasions, cuts, and insects.
- Weather-appropriate supplies, such as sunscreen and protective head covering.
- Items to entertain people during long periods of waiting—cards, word games, small games, books, or other reading material.
- Battery-operated (or hand-crank–operated) radios and other electronic items, both to provide news and information and to entertain people during long periods of waiting; spare batteries.

APPENDIX C

Suggestions on Offering Basic Spiritual First Aid

Adapted from Kevin Massey, *Light Our Way: A Guide for Spiritual Care in Times of Disaster for Disaster Response Volunteers, First Responders and Disaster Planners* (Arlington, Va.: National Voluntary Organizations Active in Disaster, 2006). Used by permission.

- Spirituality is a broader concept than religion or faith tradition. Spirituality is broader because every person has a sense of spirituality, whether he or she is "religious."
- Healthy spirituality includes a sense of awe and wonder, a sense of community, a sense of personal mission, enthusiasm for discovery and creativity, and a sense of well-being and joy.
- Symptoms of spiritual dis-ease that may occur following a disaster include reconsidering core religious beliefs, wondering about justice and meaning issues, feeling a need to be cleansed, closing oneself off from loved ones, feeling despair and hopelessness, feeling guilty, wondering about life and death, feeling shame, and asking, "Why did God do this?"
- Spiritual care consists of actions that help others draw on their own spirituality for strength, hope, and healing. In a disaster zone those who offer spiritual care may have religious beliefs very different from those receiving such care.
- Good spiritual first aid requires being present with a sense of hospitality, accepting and respecting people as they are, taking

care to avoid doing any harm. It is never appropriate to evangelize, proselytize, or exploit people who are vulnerable.

- Following a disaster people may seek spiritual care because they have lost their home, lost their business or workplace, become separated from loved ones, had a loved one die in the disaster, been seriously injured, provided immediate assistance to disaster victims, or experienced previous disasters.
- Those seeking spiritual care may also be seeking to make sense of their faith; find religious and spiritual resources; be part of a community; gain access to such essentials as food, water, and shelter; find someone who can help them feel calmer and more hopeful; find a safe person to talk with about their experiences.
- In addition to finding spiritual comfort from their places of worship and disaster chaplains, disaster victims may find it when others open their homes to relief workers or when someone offers to take over another person's work duties, so that person can care for family members hurt by the disaster; when others show community support through vigils or memorial services; or when the disaster victim experiences the spontaneous generosity of others.
- Keep what is said strictly confidential.
- Some things to say:
    - I'm sorry.
    - I'm here to help you in any way I can.
    - You have my sympathy.
    - You are in my prayers.
    - What can I do to help you?
- Remember:
    - Avoid clichés.
    - Don't be afraid to use the name of a deceased victim.
    - Don't preach or proselytize.

- › Offer prayer if requested.
- › Help people find their own solutions to the problems facing them.
- › Be cautious about giving advice.
- › Let people share their memories.
- › Don't be afraid of your own emotions.
- › Encourage people to be connected to their loved ones.

- Help individuals tap into family emotional resources for coping by encouraging them to talk about their personal history, the lives of their parents and grandparents, the history of their ethnic group, and the history of their faith group.
- Be aware of the impact that the anniversary dates of a disaster may have on survivors. Long after the initial disaster, anniversaries can trigger powerful flashback emotional reactions.
- Be aware that caregivers are susceptible to "compassion fatigue." This condition occurs when a caregiver experiences feelings of fear, pain, and suffering similar to those of the people they are helping. Reduce your risk of such fatigue by taking good care of yourself; keeping a journal; listening to soothing music; eating well; getting adequate rest, fresh air, and exercise; taking time to pray and meditate; talking openly about your own feelings; and avoiding abuse of drugs and alcohol.

APPENDIX D

The Role of the Federal Emergency Management Agency in a Disaster

On March 1, 2003, the Federal Emergency Management Agency (FEMA) became part of the U.S. Department of Homeland Security (DHS). The primary mission of the Federal Emergency Management Agency is to reduce the loss of life and property and protect the Nation from all hazards, including natural disasters, acts of terrorism, and other man-made disasters, by leading and supporting the Nation in a risk-based, comprehensive emergency management system of preparedness, protection, response, recovery, and mitigation.

—www.fema.gov

FEMA was started during President Jimmy Carter's administration. Prior to the 2003 change, FEMA functioned as an independent agency, reported directly to the president of the United States, and was fully funded and headed by a professional experienced in disaster response.

All disasters begin and end locally, but they often require more support than local structures can provide. When this is the case, systems are in place to use the resources of both the state and federal government. In a disaster, it is up to local officials to turn to the state for help and then up to state officials to turn to the federal government (FEMA) for help. In all cases, FEMA functions at the request and direction of state and local officials.

During a disaster, FEMA will participate in helping to tend to basic human needs, securing property, and beginning the process of restoring people to a functional level. They achieve these aims by:

- Providing food, water, and ice as necessary at distribution sites.
- Securing disaster sites and supporting search-and-rescue efforts.
- Helping to shore up damaged homes and buildings—"blue roofs." (As soon as possible following a disaster, damaged roofs are covered with blue tarps, which stay in place until the roofs can be replaced or repaired. The sight of "blue roofs" is one indication that one is entering a disaster area.)
- Registering people for further assistance to begin the recovery process.
- Assessing damage to structures.

FEMA assistance can come in a variety of ways, and the process is often confusing. FEMA works with the Small Business Administration (SBA) to secure funding for many disaster survivors. For those who are not eligible for an SBA loan, FEMA will help them obtain grants to begin the recovery process.

FEMA employs a cadre of people who then hand off the FEMA work to the local long-term recovery structure. These FEMA staff and voluntary agency liaisons (VALs) share FEMA data to help local long-term recovery groups plan and implement the work necessary to fill the gaps in recovery efforts. They are also experts at guiding and advising on the formation of long-term recovery efforts.

Sadly, recent disasters have generated a groundswell of negative publicity for this agency. Individual FEMA representatives generally care deeply about helping people hurt by a disaster. However, because of a combination of the overwhelming magnitude of recent disasters, the frequency of disasters in some regions, and the enormous size of the agency itself, the FEMA part of the recovery process is often cumbersome, frustrating, confusing, and upsetting to disaster victims. Congregations can help by learning the details of how the system works, helping people fill out the required forms, and providing pastoral care to those caught up in frustrating red tape.

For more information about FEMA, refer to its website at *www.fema.gov*.

Appendix E

National Nonprofit Disaster Response Organizations

NATIONAL VOLUNTARY ORGANIZATIONS ACTIVE IN DISASTER (NVOAD)

Members of National VOAD form a coalition of nonprofit organizations that respond to disasters as part of their overall mission. Together we foster more effective service through the four C's—communication, coordination, cooperation and collaboration—by providing convening mechanisms and outreach for all people and organizations involved in disasters.
—www.nvoad.org

The following list contains the names and web addresses for national nonprofit organizations linked together at a national level through National Voluntary Organizations Active in Disaster (NVOAD). Many of these organizations also have membership in state or regional Voluntary Organizations Active in Disaster (VOAD) networks. Additional organizations not listed here participate in a local or regional VOAD network, but do not qualify for membership in the National VOAD. For example, a social-service agency that serves only a specific state would be welcome at that state's VOAD network, but not qualify for membership in the NVOAD.

Adventist Community Services, *www.communityservices.org*

American Baptist Men/USA, *www.abc-usa.org*

American Radio Relay League, *www.arrl.org*

American Red Cross, *www.redcross.org*

AMURT (Ananda Marga Universal Relief Team), *www.amurt.net*

Brethren Disaster Ministries, *www.brethren.org/genbd/BDM*

Catholic Charities USA, *www.catholiccharitiesusa.org*

Christian Disaster Response International, *www.cdresponse.org*

Church World Service, *www.churchworldservice.org*

Churches of Scientology Disaster Response, *www.volunteerministers.org*

City Team Ministries, *www.cityteam.org/disasterresponse*

Convoy of Hope, *www.convoyofhope.org*

Disaster Psychiatry Outreach, *www.disasterpsych.org*

Episcopal Relief and Development, *www.er-d.org*

Feeding America (formerly America's Second Harvest), *www.feedingamerica.org*

Feed the Children, *www.feedthechildren.org*

Friends Disaster Service, Inc., *www.friendsdisasterservice.net*

Habitat for Humanity, *www.habitat.org/disaster/default.aspx*

Hope Coalition America, *www.operationhope.org/smdev//*

The Humane Society of the United States, *www.hsus.org*

International Aid, Volunteer 800.968.7490, *www.internationalaid.org*

International Critical Incident Stress Foundation, *www.icisf.org*

International Relief and Development, *www.irddc.org*

Latter Day Saints Charities, *www.lds.org*

Lutheran Disaster Response, *www.ldr.org*

Mennonite Disaster Service, *www.mds.mennonite.net*

Mercy Medical Airlift, *www.mercymedical.org*

National Association of Jewish Chaplains, *www.najc.org*

National Emergency Response Teams (NERT), *www.nert-usa.org*

National Organization for Victim Assistance, *www.trynova.org*

Operation Blessing, *www.ob.org*

Points of Light Institute and the Hands On Network, *www.handonnetwork.org*

Presbyterian Disaster Assistance, *www.pusa.org*

REACT International, Inc., *www.reactitl.org*

The Salvation Army, *www.salvationarmyusa.org*

Samaritan's Purse, *www.samaritans.org*

Save the Children, *www.savethechildren.org*

Society of St. Vincent de Paul, *www.svdpusa.org*

Southern Baptist Convention—North American Mission Board, *www.namb.net*

Taiwan Buddhist Tzu Chi Foundation USA, *www.ustzuchi.org*

United Church of Christ—Wider Church Ministries, *www.ucc.org*

United Jewish Communities, *www.ujc.org*

United Methodist Committee on Relief (UMCOR), *www.umcor.org*

United Way of America, *www.liveunited.org*

Volunteers of America, *www.voa.org*

World Vision, *www.worldvision.org*

Additional National Faith-based Organizations Responding to Disasters

The following faith-based organizations also respond to disasters but are not currently members of the National VOAD. Our thanks to Peter B. Gudatis, executive director of New York Disaster Interfaith Services, for providing names of these faith-based disaster service organizations.

Although these organizations, along with the many partner members of NVOAD, are the primary long-term disaster assistance providers, their contributions to disaster work are as varied as their spiritual practices.

American Jewish World Service (AJWS), *www.ajws.org*

Christian Contractors Association (CCA), *www.ccaministry.org*

International Orthodox Christian Charities (IOCC), *www.iocc.org*

Islamic Circle of North America-Relief (ICNA Relief), *www.reliefonline.org*

Mercy Corps, *www.mercycorps.org*

National Disaster Interfaith Network (NDIN), *www.n-din.org*

Sikh Coalition, *www.sikhcoalition.org*

United Sikhs, *www.unitedsikhs.org*

Appendix F

What to Know before You Volunteer

Based on an interview with the Rev. Kathie Bender-Schwich, assistant to the presiding bishop, Evangelical Lutheran Church in America.

Many of us feel an overwhelming urge to do something in response to news of a disaster. This natural inclination to help others is a gift and one way God surrounds us with grace in the midst of loss and panic. Like many gifts, in order to be truly beneficial to both the giver and the recipient of the gift, there are some factors to consider before we share this gift of compassion with those who need support and assistance.

- Ask yourself whose needs you are trying to meet—yours or those of the people you'll serve?
- Consider whether this type of volunteer work is the best fit for you. For example, if you tend to want to "fix things" rather than quietly listen to someone in pain, find a way to be involved that suits that inclination.
- Don't judge how disaster victims are reacting. For some, the loss of their personal things—home, car, prized possessions—is as disturbing as the death of a loved one. For others, getting out alive is such a relief that the other losses seem inconsequential. Avoid judging how or what another person grieves or appears not to be grieving.

- Don't make promises you may not be able to keep.
- Put your own needs aside to spend time listening and offering comfort for what the disaster survivor is experiencing.
- However, do take good care of yourself and avoid getting overinvolved in the other person's problems and emotions. Don't try to be a hero.
- Remember that you are there to fill a specific role. Trust that others are also helping. Disaster-response ministry is very much a team effort—even if you never meet the other members of the team.
- Take regular breaks to avoid undue stress and to put things into perspective.
- Expect the magnitude of the event to get to you, and find someone you can talk with about your experiences in the disaster zone.

APPENDIX G

Disaster-focused Time and Talent Survey

When your congregation does its annual survey of talents and interests, include a section to learn who among your members may have specific skills, contacts, or interests that could be useful in a disaster-response ministry. Be sure to collect contact information for those who complete the surveys. This list of members will be a valuable resource to share with local government and disaster-response officials if a disaster strikes your community. The following is a model for such a survey.

Can You Help?

Would you like to help respond to community needs in case of an emergency? If so, indicate the skills, experience, or training you have that could be beneficial in case of a disaster. Check all items that apply and add other skills, experiences, or training you have that may be appropriate:

Amateur radio operator (ham radio)

Cross-cultural sensitivity training

Medical training (nurses, medics, physicians, dentists, physical therapists, chiropractors, pharmacists)

Special-event coordinating

Fundraising, grant proposal writing, and other development activities

OSHA (Occupational Safety and Health administrator) guidelines or training in handling hazardous materials

Wildlife rescue experience

Animal care experience

Educators (to provide post-disaster programming or to teach pre-disaster preparedness principles)

Child-care providers

Mental-health professionals such as social workers, counselors, play therapists

Creative-arts skills such as writing, drama, music, drawing

Transportation coordination

Telecommunications skills and connections

Internet technology and computer skills

Recreational and leisure experience

Community-organizing experience

Financial management experience such as banking, loan application, budgeting

Handling insurance, working with adjusters, interpreting insurance policies, filing claims

Facilities management

Utility workers

Attorneys, paralegals, legal secretaries

Police and firefighters

Training and working with therapy pets

Construction and remodeling skills such as carpentry,

plumbing, electrical work, roofing, gardening and landscaping, painting and wallpapering

Hospitality, such as providing meals for workers or hosting people in your home

APPENDIX H

Sample Congregational Plan

A comprehensive congregational plan will address many factors and may be long. For that reason, it is difficult to include a full plan here. The list of key topics below can help guide your planning process. For further support and planning, you can work with any denomination's national disaster organization. For a complete list of these organizations, see appendix E

Introduction: Why a Disaster Plan?

Congregations can play a crucial role in helping people prepare for a disaster and organizing volunteers to respond after a disaster. However, the ability to do so requires planning. The best time to learn how disaster recovery unfolds is before a disaster happens in your community. When it comes to managing disaster recovery, the old adage about an ounce of prevention being worth a pound of cure applies.

Preparing to Mobilize

Careful planning helps congregations make the best use of their own and others' time, talents, and treasure during and after a disaster.

Response Team Members

Congregational disaster-response team members are people motivated to serve. Below are some sample job descriptions for members who might serve on a congregational disaster response team.

- *Team leader:* Calls together other disaster response team members and congregational members as appropriate to (a) assess community needs resulting from the disaster and (b) identify resources available within the congregation to meet those needs.
- *Member contact coordinator:* Oversees a system for staying in touch with individual members of the congregation. (At Emanuel, this was the Virtual Community coordinator.)
- *Communications coordinator:* Tracks incoming and outgoing phone and e-mail communications and files contact and other information for future reference.
- *Supplies coordinator:* Tracks supplies needed for response efforts, keeps inventory of supplies on hand, and finds out where to obtain required items.
- *Pastoral care coordinator:* Obtains and disseminates to disaster victims names of people qualified and available to provide spiritual and emotional support following the disaster.
- *Clean-up coordinator:* Organizes work crews that are sent out to churches, neighborhoods, or homes to clean up after the disaster.
- *Support coordinator:* Solicits and keeps track of donations of cash and in-kind gifts to ensure that construction supplies, food and lodging for volunteers, transportation, office space, and other resources are available for disaster-response workers.
- *Congregational staff support coordinator:* Oversees care for clergy and other key leaders by providing retreats away from the

disaster area, lining up other pastors to assist with the extra work, providing training to meet the demands of recovery, and so forth.

- *Property/facilities coordinator:* Facilitates setting up whatever temporary logistics might be needed for the recovery efforts, such as phones, office space, meeting rooms, and the like.

Members with Special Needs and Abilities

- Individuals with special needs: Which members will need assistance to evacuate or secure their property? Who will need immediate attention in a power failure because they have medical equipment requiring power? Which members are vulnerable because of their age or disabilities? What family members, neighbors, friends, or other caregivers should be contacted for people in any of these categories in an emergency?
- Individuals with specific abilities: Which congregational members have special training or experiences that will enable them to assist members with special needs? What specific skills does each person have? How can he or she be reached?

Community Service Organizations

Contact information for key staff and volunteers in service organizations.

Protecting Facilities, Records, and Other Assets

Depending on a variety of factors such as size, style of administration, affiliation with a national church body, and the like, each congregation establishes a routine for oversight of property, member records, and various assets. An effective congregational disaster plan will detail how the facilities, records, and other assets will be secured before a disaster and managed afterward. Define the roles and responsibilities of:

- Congregational governing board.
- Professional staff such as clergy, youth directors, music directors, and education specialists.
- Support staff such as office managers, custodial personnel, bookkeepers, and so forth.
- Other key leaders not noted above, such as treasurer, financial secretary, altar guild, and director of preschool or other key programs.

Use of the Congregation's Building as a Shelter

Congregational leaders and response team members should discuss what policies and procedures for the congregation's functioning will be needed if the building is used as a shelter.

Congregation's Role as a Spiritual Care Center

Congregational leaders and response team members should discuss how this congregation can best serve the community as a place of solace, support, and healing after a disaster.

This sample congregation disaster plan is adapted from materials in *Community Arise*, a preparedness and long term-recovery training curriculum. *Community Arise* is an ecumenical collection of educational materials available online or in print form to instruct faith-based community members how to prepare for a disaster and respond effectively following a disaster. These training materials are available at *www.communityarise.com.*

The following agencies and organizations are also good sources for information about training for disaster preparedness and response ministry:

- The websites of most denominational disaster response organizations (see appendix E).
- The American Red Cross (*www.redcross.org*).
- FEMA, which provides training materials through the Emergency Management Institute (*www.training.fema.org*). "A Citizen's Guide to Disaster Assistance" is particularly thorough and helpful for disaster training.
- Regional and local faith-based social-service agencies. Work through your denomination to locate the appropriate people and places for disaster-related materials.

APPENDIX I

A Place for All Sizes

The number of agencies and organizations involved in disaster response is large and constantly in flux. There are pros and cons to each type and size of organization.

Large Organizations

Large organizations such as the American Red Cross, FEMA, the Salvation Army, and some of the larger denominational social-service agencies and disaster-response organizations can offer:

- ***Stability.*** Even if the staff changes from disaster to disaster, there is a certain level of organizational "DNA" on which to draw, so that lessons learned in previous disasters are available to apply to the current crisis.
- ***Specialized staff.*** Since large organizations have large staffs, they typically have CEOs who can focus on strategic thinking and networking with national and regional disaster leaders. Large organizations also have staff out in the field, as well as other staff back in the office. Some can do the hands-on work of disaster response while others are out telling the story, raising the funds, and tracking the data for future reference.
- ***Financial support.*** While the levels of support for recovery efforts vary greatly from disaster to disaster, large organizations generally have a very large and well-developed donor

database on which to draw, financial reserves, and specialized staff people who know how to raise money and apply for grants.

- ***Name recognition.*** Large-scale organizations can afford to do the kind of public relations and development projects that result in media coverage, appeal to celebrities who endorse and support their mission, and allow upper-level management to network with local, regional, and national decision makers in government.

However, these advantages come with a downside. Some of the disadvantages:

- ***Slowly, but surely.*** Large organizations may require days or weeks or even months before they are able to respond fully to the aftermath of a disaster. A large organization may also be involved simultaneously in several disasters in multiple areas. This means no one disaster is the "only child" calling out for the attention of the responders.
- ***Growing pains.*** Nonprofit organizations of any size depend on donor dollars as a significant part of the operating budget. When the donations are up, the size of the staff expands. When donations drop, staff must be reduced or reassigned. These staffing changes can make people in the disaster zone feel abandoned or frustrated as those they counted on for help are no longer available to them.
- ***Too big?*** In a large organization it is common for the field staff to feel disconnected from the home office staff. For example, a field staff worker clearly sees an immediate need to buy more materials so that volunteers can keep doing roof repairs for an elderly couple living with buckets and plastic sheeting everywhere. The home-office person responsible for writing checks and approving the expenditures within a

predetermined budget may be several hundred miles removed from the leaking roof and unable to sense the urgency of the situation. Funds don't always flow freely or quickly through large organizations.

Life in the Middle

Midsize organizations tend to be entities such as denominational judicatory districts, or county or regional social-service or governmental organizations that were put in place long before the disaster. Following a disaster they may add oversight for disaster-recovery efforts to a list of other functions. The advantages of midsize organizations are:

- ***Familiarity with the people and other organizations in the region.*** Especially within the faith-based community, these midsize organizations most likely have a history with congregations from having done other types of work together. The informal networks are probably rather well developed. People know one another and have a sense of the gifts and passions of one another.
- ***Access to people with resources.*** These midsize organizations probably already know who has money to spare and who is most likely to share those funds. They may have a history of raising funds for other group efforts, such as conferences, or hosting special events for youth.
- ***Small but experienced staff.*** Midsize organizations typically have just enough staff to provide professional leadership that can move about within the disaster region, both to assess needs and to bring reassurance to those struggling. And they still have some staff back at the office responding to phone calls, e-mails, and the paperwork that will no doubt be part of the recovery work.

The disadvantages of being a midsize organization might include:

- ***Role confusion.*** It is sometimes difficult for midsize agencies to clarify how they fit in. They don't have the resources of the large organizations, and they aren't operating primarily at the site of the disaster. Staff may easily duplicate efforts of other disaster agencies or fail to respond because they assume other organizations are taking care of the matter.
- ***Compassion fatigue.*** Because responding to disasters is not the primary focus or mission of a regional organization, the staff who get involved in this work may burn out rather quickly. Many a well-intentioned compassionate person has rushed in ill-prepared to manage the seemingly never-ending list of problems, people in acute pain and depression, and hours of meetings required to stay on top of the disaster-recovery work. However, having now established a reputation for being "the person to talk to about that," one may find it difficult to back out of disaster work graciously to get back to other work.

The Least of These

Disasters draw out creativity and determination. People living in the disaster zone see needs that no one seems to be doing anything about and so quickly form a group to meet those needs. New agencies regularly crop up in the wake of a disaster. For example, the Gulf Coast now has entrepreneurs advertising their services to help homeowners file disputes with insurance companies over how much compensation they received for storm-related property damages. Many a nonprofit organization was born as a result of a disaster.

The advantages of these small organizations:

- ***Effective leadership.*** They are generally headed by passionate and determined local people who have energy and knowledge of how their community works. They know who's who and how to get into the offices of the people who make the decisions locally. Or they have the determination to find out.

- ***Action and attraction.*** They are able to move quickly and attract others who want to join their cause.
- ***Experience-based understanding.*** They do know exactly how people are struggling, because they are disaster victims themselves or are surely living with or next to others who are.

The disadvantages:

- ***Small operations.*** They are usually one-person or at the most two- or three-person operations. The CEO is also the person who opens and closes the office (if there is one), raises and disburses the funds, and does most of whatever work gets done.
- ***One-shot organizations.*** Once the disaster-recovery work winds down, they become organizations without a cause. They must then either find another disaster to get involved with or disband.

Why Size Matters

Congregational leaders need to understand how different sizes of organizations function in disaster-recovery work. Not understanding this factor can leave people with unrealistic expectations about what the agency and its staff "should" be doing. The unrealistic expectations then lead to frustration, bitterness, resentment, depression, and at times even rage and hostile actions when an organization and the people representing it do not or cannot respond as anticipated.

These unfulfilled expectations can result in what amounts to a community "meltdown." Disillusioned people may have strong but ultimately unproductive outbursts, because they didn't understand or couldn't accept the various capabilities and roles of the responding organizations. Thus, people who are already highly stressed from the terrible experiences of the disaster may begin to feel victimized again by a system that just doesn't seem to care or respond.

Congregational disaster-preparedness efforts can do much to mitigate this unfortunate additional stress. Congregations can fill an important role by teaching people in advance what to expect and, equally important, what not to expect.

Expect the unexpected. Be flexible. Get educated. Get acquainted with the disaster-response people and organizations within your denomination and community *before* a disaster occurs.